PHOTOGRAPHS BY DANIEL LAINÉ

AFRICAN GODS

Contemporary Rituals and Beliefs

Preface by Tobie Nathan
Essays by Anne Stamm and Pierre Saulnier

Flammarion

Translated from the French by Susan Pickford

Copyediting: Anne Korkeakivi

Design: Stéphane Thidet

Typesetting: Claude-Olivier Four

Proofreading: Penny Isaac

Color Separation: Artisans du regard, Paris

Distributed in North America by Rizzoli International Publications, Inc.

Simultaneously published in French as *Dieux Noirs*

© Flammarion, Paris, 2007

English-language edition

© Flammarion, 2007

87, quai Panhard et Levassor

75647 Paris Cedex 13

www.editions.flammarion.com

07 08 09   3 2 1

ISBN 978-2-0803-0019-5

Dépôt légal: 07/2007

Printed in Singapore by Imago

CONTENTS

FOR THE BAMILEKE,
DEATH DOES NOT EXIST

When the Bamileke of Cameroon die, they are elevated to the title of ancestor only if they have had children. Infertile couples and the unmarried cannot become ancestors. For an ancestor to defend the family against evil spirits, his descendants must possess the ancestor's skull. The skull of a deceased relative is dug up several months after burial and kept in a sacred place, guarded by the legitimate heir of the family lineage. Only human skulls have the power to communicate with higher powers and enter into spiritual contact with the soul of the deceased. Such spiritual contact can be used to grant a wish or to make a request of Si, the creator. Because, for the Bamileke, death does not exist: the soul simply leaves the body to continue its life within the world of ancestors. After a certain time, it is reincarnated in another member of the family. Some families clearly recognize in their children the behavior and attitudes of some long-deceased ancestor.

The Bamileke believe in reincarnation. Some have perfect recall of their former lives, particularly the most recent. They refer to the experiences of their past lives spontaneously, which sometimes leads their families to mistrust or even fear them.

Banjoun, Cameroon

FOREWORD

Tobie Nathan

RELIGION

Religion enshrines and crystallizes human intelligence. It is an inextricable blend of history, politics, and the awareness of belonging to a community. It accompanies individuals in the most intense experiences of their lives. It is both public knowledge, available to all, and composed of esoteric secrets hidden from the unordained. But, above all, religion means a shared belief in divinity. It fleshes out the divine's image, establishes the rules of relations between the divine and mortals, and defines the obligations men owe the divine and the boons and blessings men can expect in return.

In Africa, probably more than elsewhere, religions have focused shared belief in divinity on invisible beings and ways of rising above the mortal world. Traditional African religions apotheosize the hidden depths of everyday life, in a way that is very hard for anyone accustomed to the modern, rule-bound form taken by mainstream religion in Europe and the United States to understand.

Anthropologists and historians often use the term "animist" to refer to traditional African religions, suggesting that they are no more than the naive attribution of anthropomorphic intentions and motivations to natural elements and events. However, followers of these religions are able to contemplate the countenance, touch the body, and experience in a concrete manner the energy of their gods.

The communities that nineteenth-century anthropologists referred to as "ethnic groups" are still very important in modern-day Africa. An ethnic group may be defined as a community linked by a common language, land, and/or religious belief, such as the Yoruba in Benin and Nigeria, the Ibo in Nigeria, the Mina and Ewe in Togo, the Fang in Gabon, the Ashanti in Ghana, the Akan peoples in Ivory Coast, the Mossi and Bobo in Burkina Faso, and the Bakongo in the Congo.

There are literally hundreds of languages and peoples in Africa—some fifty in Ivory Coast, Benin, and Togo, and over two hundred each in Congo and Nigeria. These groups, whose histories are often neglected, still have widespread influence over daily life and social institutions in modern-day Africa. Political parties often follow tribal lines, while traditional practices governing individual protection and conflict management still play a major role in the organization of African societies in all areas of modern life, including public life, business, and elections.

MAKING GODS

There are countless traditional African religions, their myths passed down orally from generation to generation, although such oral traditions are now being relegated to the shadows by the presence in Africa of the great monotheistic religions of Christianity and Islam. These traditional religions include Bwiti, practiced by the Fang in Gabon; Ndop, practiced by the Lebou in Senegal; and Bori, practiced by the Hausa in Niger. The Yoruba, a community of twenty million people who live mainly in southern Nigeria and Benin, follow the faith known as Orisha, or Vodun elsewhere. It spread worldwide in past centuries along the routes of the slave trade and has continued to gain followers outside the African continent ever since. Today, Vodun has many believers in the West Indies, in Haiti (where it is known as *vaudou*, or voodoo), and Cuba (where it is known as *santeria*). Under the appellation *candomble*, it is also well-known in Brazil, particularly in predominantly black cities such as Salvador de Bahia and Rio de Janeiro. It is practiced in the southern United States too, in the states of Louisiana and Florida (as voodoo), as well as further north, in New York, and even in Montreal in Canada. The number of Vodun worshippers worldwide is estimated at some 60 million, compared to 2.6 billion Christians, 1.3 billion Muslims, one billion Hindus, 325 million Buddhists, 230 million Taoists, and 15 million Jews.

What is a *vodun*? Certainly, this is the name of the Vodun deity. But Vodun is equally the rite in which this deity is worshipped, its congregation, and the ritual-based techniques that help its worshippers in their daily lives to protect themselves, treat ill health, and face adversity—or adversaries.

Vodun represents a special sense of oneness. It is unity, and is imbued with the ability to transform the manifold elements of its composition into one. The physical manifestation of the god can be constructed from all sorts of materials. The Ondo vodun in the town of Pobé, for example, takes the form of wooden stakes, driven into the ground and surrounded with metal blades. Legba voduns are rough clay statues, sometimes with an enormous erect phallus, sometimes studded with metal spikes. The Dan vodun takes the form of earthenware jars and vases, filled with liquids and other materials that remain a mystery to the uninitiated. The chief vodun of the town of Ouidah is a shapeless heap of sand and earth, surrounded by a brightly colored satin ribbon.

The vodun is fed by sacrificing animals and sprinkling their blood over the altar, as well as with ritual libations of four vital drinks: colorless spirits such as rum or gin (or, in Benin, a traditional palm wine distillation called *sodabi*); palm wine or banana beer; a sugary drink such as Coca-Cola or Fanta; and plain water. It is constantly being rebuilt as well, as worshippers daily add new elements and material, such as red palm oil and earth, to it. Built of an erratic

THE *HOGON* FORGOES PHYSICAL CONTACT

The *hogon* is the priest of the deity Lebe, the old-man serpent. Every night, the sacred snake visits him and licks his body. The snake's saliva contains a magic force that gives the priest the strength to live another day. The hogon must not wash or sweat; if he does he will lose the magic power of Lebe. The day when the hogon is frightened by the snake, he dies.

Lebe Seru, the first Dogon ancestor, took the form of a snake to guide his people to the Bandiagara cliffs in Mali. In each village, an altar was built out of soil from the ancestral homeland mixed with soil from the new country. This is how Lebe began to be worshipped.

The hogon oversees the religious and farming rites that allow the Dogon people to cultivate the soil and to have children. In general, the hogon is the oldest man in the village. It is not a role to which a future hogon aspires. The decision is taken in his absence, and then the next hogon is informed of his new duty. Once he has been given the role, the hogon's daily life comes to an end, and he must follow a strict set of rules. He is no longer allowed the least physical contact with others. No one is allowed to shake his hand, for example, not even his wife and children. He must forswear sexual intercourse. He cannot touch the ground with his bare feet. He lives a solitary life, not leaving his home, and is only allowed to receive visitors and preside over village meetings.

Bandiagara, Mali

mix of objects, recipient of human prayers always spoken aloud and of daily attentions by believers, it takes on life and becomes the god. It is warm and soft to the touch. Believers can see it move. It speaks through the mouth of worshippers, making predictions, handing out advice, and giving orders. The intelligence of traditional African religions lies in the intricate relationship it creates between humans and the divine: it is because the vodun is built by humans that it is alive. Worshippers know that because they make their gods from wood, iron, earth, blood, fire, and water, the gods in return make men, granting them a share of their vital energy, crystallized in the power of creation.

A MULTIPLICITY OF GODS

In Africa, traditional religious thought is governed by certain principles. There is a multiplicity of gods. There may have been one single god at the origin of the world, but he is represented as pre-existing the world and beyond human reach. This primordial god, whose name is typically the same as the one used for God in translations of the Bible (for example, Mawu or Mawu-Lisa in the Fon language of Benin) is a figure of desolation and melancholy. It is as though, for Africans, monotheism is the religion of the Creation, but it was such a sad religion that God himself decided to move on. In the beginning, the original Yoruba god, Olodumare, was bored. He was simultaneously world and intention, matter and desire. He existed beyond time, in a compact undifferentiated totality. So bored was he in this state that he decided, so the story goes, to make existence's first sacrifice by splitting himself in two. Seven gods sprang from the half he removed. He divided them into two groups, the first six on one side and the seventh, Legba (or, to give him his whole name, Eshu Elegbara) on the other. They were all perched on a palm tree rooted in the depths of the ocean, surrounded by the waves. The first six were on one frond, the seventh on another.

Among the first were Shango, god of war; Ogun, god of the forge; Avrekete, silken-haired goddess of the sea, known in Brazil as Iemanja and throughout Africa as Mami Wata (Mammy Water); and Omolu, often called Sakpata. This was the beginning of the beginning, the time before time, when there was no space to allow time to expand. Up above, God was the vault of the sky, and beneath him was nothing but water. From the heart of the waves, he brought forth a kind of palm tree that bears nuts with two pairs of eyes, the same nuts used as aids in the divination ritual known as *Fa*, or *Afa*. He helped the deities down with a rope, and each went to huddle on a separate branch, solitary and silent, not even knowing how to speak to each other. Followers of traditional Africa religions believe that, although the gods embody power, they are condemned to noncommunicativeness.

Olodumare then assigned elements to these first new gods: Shango the terrible was entrusted with lightning, thunder, and stones; Ogun, with the forge and iron weaponry; Omolu the indispensable, with smallpox and other infectious diseases. They now controlled powerful elements, and they remained alone on their branches, jealously protecting their powers. The primordial god no doubt felt some disappointment when he saw that the deities he had just created were settling into the same state of melancholy solitude that he had rebelled against. That is why he chose to give nothing to Oronyia, as Legba is also known, the seventh and youngest deity, except for a mysterious object, both dark and light at the same time. The harder you throw this object, as the story is told in Benin, the closer to you it falls. It is a kind of stone, whose strange name can be translated as "black/eyes open." This stone fell from Legba's hand, and where it fell is where the earth began. Only then did the other deities, the voduns, climb down from the palm tree, and life could begin.

The multiplicity of deities in the Yoruba pantheon is reflected in the multiplicity of human forms, which are composite and created from a variety of elements, some originating in the cosmos and others inherited from human ancestors. The diversity of the human's origins creates a mosaic personality. The following is the Yoruban myth of human creation. According to the Ancients, the supreme god—known by the names Olodumare, Olorun, or Mawu in different parts of Yoruba, Fon, Ewe, and Gun territory—entrusted the lesser gods with the task of creating the various parts of the human body, which they molded from sand. In the beginning, men were, therefore, formed one by one, from whatever was on hand, and shaped according to the whims of the gods. Then, Eshu Elegbara (Legba), the god of crossroads and openings and, therefore, of potential, chose a moment when his father was distracted to poke a hole in the human bodies, thereby creating sexuality. Legba, thus, relieved the gods of their burden, by allowing a mechanical means to reproduce the same model over and over again.

The Mandingo people of Mali and Guinea, who founded the vast Mali Empire under the leadership of Sundiata Keita, had their own creation myth. They believe, as do many other peoples in West Africa, that the first humans were pairs of twins. Every individual, in other words, had a double, which today they call a *jinna* (from the Arabic word *jinn*). Men chose to live in hierarchical village communities with their families and honor their ancestors and relatives. In short, they created civilization. *Jinna*, on the other hand, chose to live in the bush, rivers, forests, and treetops, in chaos. Men chose to live in an ordered but sterile world, while *jinna* preferred a world of excess, abundance, profusion, and fecundity. *Jinna* were the guardians of life principles, vital

BLUE, THE COLOR OF RITUAL DEATH

In Africa, blue is a negative color representing cold, but also purity, dreams, and earthly rest. For these young Kota, it represents the ritualistic burial of their youth and entry into manhood. They are part of an all-male secret society, the largest in Africa, called Mungala, whose members hold initiation ceremonies for young men and play an important social role in villages by protecting crops and resolving disputes.

Congo

forces, fertility, and reproduction, while men were the guardians of the past, memory, and language.

But, the question remained of how to build a world to last. What could be done to prevent men's tendency to organize everything around him from returning the world to the sheer tedium of its uniformity at the moment of creation? Every time men had to call on the forces of life, they had to renegotiate the terms of their original alliance with their *jinna*. At the birth of a child, they removed what they called "the little brother," or "the twin" (the placenta) and returned it to where it belonged, in the bush. They made offerings of blood for weddings, when a new house was built, at harvest time, and to bring on the rains. If a woman neglected to make the gift of her placenta to the *jinna* in thanks for her fertility, the *jinna* would come and take it by force, depriving the woman of her hard-won potential to give life—what the Wolof of Senegal call her *fit*. A woman's *fit* is not her blood, but the energy in the blood which heats her body and controls her moods.

This myth is, doubtless, at the roots of a belief found throughout Africa, both in traditional religions and in Muslim and Christian communities, that animal sacrifices purify the world, washing away corruption and recreating life. Youssouf Cissé recounts the Bambara belief that, in the beginning, God cleansed the world by sacrificing "the eminent ram of the eminent master of the heavens."[1]

SHARING THE BODY

In exchange for their incursions into the realm of the gods, men ritually offer their bodies to the deities. For, while the gods represent intentions, desire, will, and strength, men represent physical being. It is, therefore, natural for the two to come together from time to time. The Yoruba believe that every man has his own deity, but the degree of familiarity depends on the individual. For some, the deity called vodun (*orisha* to the Yorubas, and *vodu* to the Ewe, the Mina, and the Fon) is no more than a protective entity to be honored in ritual. For others, the deity is a constitutive part of the individual's identity. Some believe that the deity shares every aspect of life, even the most private. These people are consecrated to their deity, sometimes from a very early age. They live in a sacred space, a kind of convent, where they remain for years, sometimes even decades. There, they learn to welcome the deity, and to let the god take possession of their body and control its movements and speech. They learn a secret language that enables them to communicate with invisible forces and songs to placate the gods.

Anyone walking through the streets of Abomey, Alada, or Porto-Novo might see processions of worshippers dressed as vodun, dancing through the streets to the sound of drums. Each dance step follows the footsteps of the god, and the dancers speak a divine language and sing hymns to invite the god to join their celebration and enjoy the company of men.

In the 1980s, Mathieu Kérékou, president of Benin, was inspired by Marxist-Leninist ideology to try to eradicate this ancestral "opium of the people." He believed its traditions to be incompatible with a modern state. The people of Benin tell how the vodun fled to the bush to hide. But, in 1986, when the followers of Shango came out of hiding, a wind more violent than anyone had ever seen devastated the country's main port, Cotonou, tearing the roofs off houses and knocking down the half-built walls found throughout the city as if they were made of straw. The people of Benin were seized with terror, including the khaki-wearing Maoist civil servants espousing the new theories of eclectic materialism. The *babalawos* (masters of the secret) came out of the bush, the musicians left the sacred grove, and the gods began to dance once more.

The communist leadership attacked the heart and soul of the Yoruba with all the arguments at their command. They wanted to "fight against obscurantism and retrograde practices." Certain rites were simply too expensive, they claimed, and were a shameful exploitation of the poor. But the *babalawos* are not also called "masters of the night" for nothing. One fine night in 1990, the people of Benin gathered together in joyous crowds to take the statue of Lenin to the port, where it was put on a ship to be taken back to Russia. As they did so, they sang, "Lenin, you are a bad boy, go home to your parents!"

TWINS

As a global average, one in eighty births produces twins. In Africa, the proportion rises to one in twenty. It is a mystery of genetics. Africans have always considered that birth consists in separating the baby from its double, or "little brother," the placenta. When the double takes the form of a twin birth, it is as if the order of the world were testing its limits, demanding a gesture of reparation to separate the physical and spiritual worlds. It may be the case that, in the past, in some places, one or both of the twins was put to death.

A legend recounts how one day the Fa oracle ordered men to stop killing the second twin and instead to honor twins as deities come down to earth. Whatever the case, many Africans are still highly ambivalent about twin births. Twins are reputed to have supernatural, independent, and antagonistic powers. They could leave to join a community of twins, splitting off from the main community. They must be forced to share with the rest of the family,

SEXUAL INTERCOURSE AS MYSTICAL EXPRESSION

During Fela Kuti concerts, dancers had a special role. They were shut in cages in the four corners of the room, above the audience. They were covered head to toe with ritual body paint and were not permitted to stop dancing until they fell into a trance. They had to be possessed by the music. The singer's goal was to create a mystical state in his dancers through physical movement. He wanted them to inspire the audience to have sexual intercourse, which he called "the expression of God."

Lagos, Nigeria

clan, and lineage. Their birth is marked by celebrations, they are given prestigious names, their mother's name is changed to "mother of twins," and the next child to be born to the mother is also linked to their special status.

In Yoruba, twins are called *ibeji* (twice-born), from *ibe* meaning "birth" and *ji* meaning "two." Twins are, therefore, one person in two bodies. If one of the twins dies, the parents must consult the *babalawo*, who will undoubtedly order them to carve a wooden statuette to become a receptacle for the dead twin's being. This statuette will receive the same care and attention as the surviving twin. It will be washed with him and then rubbed with red oil that, over time, will give it a particular patina only found in *ibeji* statues. When the surviving twin is breastfed, the statue is held to the other nipple. The mother dresses it and carries it tied to her back with a cloth like a baby. In return, she will ask favors of the *ibeji*. These statues, now popular with collectors in the West, are often marked with cuts and grooves. This is because when a member of the family falls ill or has an accident, the dead twin will be called on to help. Shavings have likely been cut from the sacred statue to be ground into powder for use as an ingredient in traditional medicines.

CELESTIAL CHRISTIANITY

Gbigbowiwe (white breath) is a term used by Fon followers of the Church of Celestial Christianity to refer to their purity of soul. The number of African Christians affiliated to one or another of the numerous independent Christian churches founded by black prophets is estimated to be over sixty million. There may be as many as ten thousand of these independent churches, making them a major phenomenon. The Church of Celestial Christianity—one of the Aladura (owners of prayer, in Yoruba) movement of churches—was founded in 1947 by Samuel Biléou Joseph Oschoffa in Porto-Novo, Benin. Samuel Oschoffa was a carpenter, pastor, and prophet.

Such African Christian churches define themselves as bastions against witchcraft and traditional Vodun-style religions. However, these churches also often provide a refuge for ancestral beliefs rejected by modernity.

One such church is the Church of Celestial Christianity in the Parish of Akpakpa-Centre in Cotonou. Services take place in a small room, ten-by-thirteen feet, with bare concrete walls. In the sparsely furnished space there are crucifixes, a few religious images, two or three prayer books, fruit, doubtless left there as offerings, and some empty bottles and cardboard boxes scattered on the floor. In the center, there is a pinewood table and some chairs that didn't match. A slow fan silently spinning on the ceiling is the one element of luxury. The Church of Celestial Christianity plays a social role,

problems, and providing hospitality, warmth, and social activities comparabl to those found in the native villages of these families, who form part of th great rural exodus happening across Africa.

The services practiced here are Christian—obsessively so—but the spir of Vodun is, nonetheless, present in its use of trances, candles, anointmen with oils, heady incense, and "Saint Michael's perfume," which cannot b found anywhere else. Traditional religion is constantly evoked also by the wa leaders of the service call stridently on each worshipper to combat Satan an the witches who hide in the midst of society. It is even whispered that th anointing oil smells strangely of fish—which is hardly surprising if, as i rumored, it is made from python fat. A python called Dan is the vodun of th Fon and Yoruba of the Ouidah region. Either the *gbigbowiwes* are hiding thei vodun in the church without their believers knowing, or they are drawing o the ancestral strength of the vodun for the sake of their new religion.

Modern African churches, which are generally classified as sects in th West, are a new phenomenon, unlike anything found elsewhere in the worlc People go to them to pray and to regroup in order to form new social force that, although thoroughly African, are more compatible with a globalizec world. People talk politics, sometimes even war, and come to seek comfor away from the harsh solitude of modern city life.

Ouidah, about ten o'clock on a Sunday morning. An astonishing sight in th streets. Mass has just finished. Crowds of believers, families together, spill ou of the grand cathedral. They cross the road to the Church of the Python, small building, long and thin, restored as part of the "Ouidah 92" festivities There, they offer libations and seek assistance from their ancestral voduns Sometimes they pick up the church's inhabitants—pythons, dry and hard as the tree roots they resemble, some as long as ten feet.

As Ouidah goes about its daily business under the merciless sun, th voduns, rare among more modern gods, once again demonstrate thei capacity to share the world with gods from elsewhere.

WESTERNERS ARE CONSIDERED UGLY

This woman taking part in a Vodun ceremony is wearing a ritual mask symbolizing Westerners. The vodun-si (vodun-wife) uses the mask as protection against those evil spirits that do not dare attack white people, who represent power and wealth for many Africans, who fear and respect them. Westerners are always shown in the statuettes known as *colons* (colonists, from the French) with a hard expression and a stiff pose. During colonization, Westerners were reputed to be brutal, deceitful, clumsy, naive, and stupid. Above all, they were thought to be terribly ugly. This made them all the more frightening.

Togo

AFRICAN RELIGIONS

Anne Stamm

Throughout the photographs in this book it is noticeable how the subject's gaze is turned inward or fixed on a vague nothingness, as though few of the people photographed seem to be taking notice of the photographer. Many seem completely uninterested in the onlooker or, indeed, in the external, material world as a whole.

Shaped as we are by our rationality, we find it hard to enter a world where ecstasy battles for supremacy with a kind of subconscious vacuum, a space filled with music and movement, where dance itself is meaningful and open to different degrees of interpretation, according to the level of awareness of the participants.

Like all great religious institutions, African religions aim to extend the experience of their followers from the outer to the inner world. They do so by a variety of means: words, gestures, sounds, and elements of nature. As the poet and former Senegalese president Léopold Sédar Senghor wrote, "For Black Africans, everything is a sign and a meaning, even abstractions and numbers, although they are thoroughly cultural values." These symbols, created for men by men, aim to make it easier to access all or part of a field that is unknown, perhaps even dangerous, even to those otherwise condemned by their weak intellect to remain outside the field of knowledge. The human personality is understood not as a closed system shut off from the outside world but as an element capable of being at one with its surroundings.

The photographs in this book come from a wide range of societies. Some of these societies have been in contact with foreign ways of thinking for centuries, and the apparent indifference of the people photographed could be seen as an indication of hostility and a desire to thwart any challenge to their power. Others have never been in contact with other societies and are, nonetheless, prey to the internal conflicts that characterize all social groups, their apparent indifference revealing their use of transcendence as a way of overcoming minor, and sometimes even much more serious, disputes.

In these societies, "the supernatural is an experience inherent in social life, inseparable from what is lived and seen,"[2] but which is only revealed if the person for whom the revelations were intended asks a direct question. In Africa, such questions are expected. The answers are given partially, without revealing all, to enable the asker to follow up with further questions and to explore what he has been told by himself. Such questions allow the asker to grow in awareness and even reach the stage of illumination.

As Dominique Zahan writes, "the stages of initiation are remarkably similar in societies that are otherwise extremely different."[3] He believes that they result in the creation of the *Homo socialis*, who is a "closed being." Even the exuberance of dancing, music, and songs of possession is not about externalizing one's most private self but, rather, expressing one's discomfort and dependence on a particular god or spirit, in a form that appears uncontrolled and uncontrollable but does, in fact, follow a strict canon, whose patterns and their possible variants all participants know by heart.

As Luc de Heusch writes, possession is "one way of getting closer to the divine through more or less violent techniques leading to ecstasy." The first crisis of possession can be the attack of an evil spirit, the sudden intrusion of an ancestor in need of a steed or a wife, or it can be a slow penetration that appears non-violent, but which can cause death if not channeled. It is used to soothe troubles or to resolve conflicts. It is important to teach those believers chosen for possession the musical and physical techniques that will allow them to live through periods of possession without danger and that will enable them to contribute to the community by becoming a living temple to the powers of light.

The chosen few are often men and, even more often, women with special healing powers. They are typically excellent herbalists, who have studied their natural surroundings in great depth. They are also skilled psychologists who succeed in resolving whatever is upsetting the harmony of the group in a highly institutional and normalized manner. They generally know how to use spirits as guardians of traditional values, at the same time as assuring that the moments of possession they manage coexist in harmony with the dominant religion, be it Islam or Christianity. In all cases, they can be seen as sorts of secondary deities who represent a link with one greater god, who is too distant to intervene in human affairs and is not worshipped directly, but who delegates part of his powers to spirits or noteworthy ancestors. All these figures represent the countless gods of the pantheon. Such gods are constantly appearing, while others die and are reincarnated.

It is difficult to classify these spirits as good or evil, because—in Nigeria, for example—a spirit that is reputed to be good, can become bad. The god of the harvest, for example, can cause crops to fail, women to become infertile, and men impotent, but his protection brings health. All gods can potentially strike without warning, and for those adversely affected—victims of illness—the only solution is to be initiated into that religion by becoming the "mare," or the wife, of the god.

WITCHES HAVE FOUR EYES

Given the status of women throughout most of Africa, there is one realm in which they can wield considerable power: witchcraft. During daylight hours, women's responsibilities are traditionally domestic, and center on the home and the family. Throughout most African countries, such work is held in low regard, and is literally considered "impure." After dark, these perceived "impure" activities metamorphose into the practice of witchcraft. According to local beliefs, witches have four eyes to allow them to see in the dark and to see the spirits that walk the earth. It is also believed that witches can split their body and soul in two, allowing them to commit nefarious deeds while the physical body remains asleep.

Lagos, Nigeria

When the spirit demands, the person possessed must take on the role of the possessing spirit so that all present can recognize it. Occasionally, the spirits are masked by Christian alter egos, because the pagan pantheon was discouraged during colonization. Thus, family altars sometimes feature the Virgin Mary, Saint Patrick, Saint James, John the Baptist, or Saint Joseph, along with their attributes: the bleeding heart, color, saber, ram, and old man. They stand alongside the ancestors and give them credibility.

Rituals vary from place to place, but the ceremonies share enough common characteristics for worshippers from other churches to follow, either because of the attire of those participating, or the music that accompanies and often triggers their periods of possession. The whole congregation can assist the incarnation of the god or spirit by chanting and singing, playing their own role in the ceremony along with the person possessed.

The ceremony is over when the person possessed has delivered their message in the voice and gestures of the spirit—male or female—inhabiting their body. Sometimes, the healer collapses in exhaustion and needs help to come to. In this case, they are entrusted to what in West Africa are called "calm women," who have learned how to bring people down from high emotional excitement to a state of calm, or even despondency.

These ceremonies of possession may appear chaotic to Western eyes, but this is far from the case for the groups amidst which they take place, who are thoroughly familiar with their patterns, from the initial rituals to the litanies, possession, messages, sacrifices (which do not take place at every service), and prophesies. While cultural communities certainly are independent from one another, the forms of worship are maintained by a process of initiation handed down from generation to generation. This process is plainer and shorter for a simple worshipper than for a priest. Priests only master their duties of divination by a long process of apprenticeship that can last for several years.

In order to cure the physically and mentally ill, the healer must reach a diagnosis and discover which spirit or god is responsible for the sickness. The healer must, therefore, be able to read the past and present. To do this, the healer will consult a soothsayer. Soothsayers are intelligent, have a thorough knowledge of their communities, and believe themselves to be possessed by a transcendent being. Once the diagnosis has been made, he passes the information on to the healer, doctor, or magician, unless he himself fulfils one of these roles.

The soothsayer is a major figure in African society. As Dominique Zahan writes, he masters the art of entering the world of signs and, reading them by his own method, uses the signs to shed light on a given situation. There are many different ways of practicing divination. The soothsayer draws his knowledge from himself or from what he is given to interpret. In either case, he sees himself as the voice of the supernatural world and of fate. His role is that of a prophet, whose incantations influence not only those who come to consult but the wider social community. Seers receive divine inspiration during crises of possession as well as through more rational methods. The seer presents himself in front of an audience, each member of which can, rightly or wrongly, come to their own conclusions. The answers given are always ambiguous, drawing on different layers of symbolic meaning inspired by the community's way of thinking, language, and beliefs.

Seers need material to read. The Bantu of southeastern Africa use anklebones, while the Dogon use drawings based on jackal spoor. Cowry shells are used all over sub-Saharan Africa. Seers can use their hands, statuettes, spiderwebs, the death throes of baby birds, needles, calabashes of water, and so on. According to Dominique Zahan, such practices of divination are based on the psychological notion of the existence of the alter ego and its mobility, as opposed to the immobility of the soul, which only leaves the body at the moment of death.

Seers enter into things and beings. They become the world, living through the people who come to consult them and the society in which they live, which in turn live through them. This explains the eminent position held by seers in traditional African societies.

Once the seer has analyzed the ill afflicting an individual or a group, he recommends that the person or group consult one of the specialists that African societies have created. He must send the individual to see a healer if required. The healer's role is as much to reassure as to cure. He is familiar with plants, infusions, and poultices, which he must prepare with incantations and dances and whose aim is to soothe, distract, and ward off all sorts of afflictions and fears.

Learning these skills and medical and botanical techniques takes many long years of effort. Reputed healers are always followed by one or more pupils, who act not only as servants but also study skills and techniques that are not to be learned in any book. The fundamental principles of the healer's traditional medicine are opposition and similarity. Apprentice healers are never taught which plants to pick before their initiation, for which they are sometimes required to pay large sums of money. They must have deep knowledge of human psychology and character, and of the local families, their alliances and vendettas, and the conflicts that set them more or less openly against each other.

THE SYMBOLISM OF BEADS

This young Baluba boy is the clan chieftain's son. He is wearing a cardboard crown to indicate his social rank, during what was formerly the Zairean national holiday. His rank is not affected by his poverty. His beads represent his home community. Each of his beads symbolizes his bond with the other members of his family and indicate that he is a member of the chief's clan. The beads are potent symbols in other ways: losing a bead is a harbinger of a death in the family, and if the boy dreams of threading beads, he is likely to be married by the end of the year. In central Africa, beads represent spiritual wellbeing rather than material wealth. When a Baluba dies, the priests place a few beads in his hands so that he can pay for his journey into the afterlife.

Democratic Republic of Congo

These same rules govern the world of magic and witchcraft. Magicians practice their craft openly by day. They bear their insignia proudly, very often wearing a tail as a symbol of power, using it to point out witches responsible for causing disruption in the community. Witches, on the other hand, act at night, hidden from prying eyes, to carry out their nefarious deeds. Sometimes, witches reveal themselves in a great flurry of terrifying, even repulsive signs. They are on the side of evil, of darkness, of what the Bambara call the "great death," of ill-gotten knowledge, and of women, who are always a source of anxiety to men. Magicians, on the other hand, are in the service of good, daylight, social cohesion, and stability. Their main role is to hunt out witches. Their dance is held to be a very effective means of protection and the best way to obtain extraordinary powers. They protect victims from being cannibalized by witches, a fate which would entail first being turned into an animal. Children cannot be considered witches, even if it later turns out that they carry in them the burden of witchcraft, handed down to them by their mothers. Witchcraft only becomes apparent in adulthood. Women are very frequently accused of witchcraft, particularly if they are seen to be changeable or do not let themselves be controlled. They are considered to be like the night or shadows, impossible to grasp.

When a seer or a magician detects an act of witchcraft, the whole village gathers together to take part in a social performance that will lead to the discovery of the witches' magic charms, which are more or less hidden. The gathering ends with the destruction of the charms in front of—and with the active involvement of—the crowd. It does not matter that the charms, amulets, or other objects may, in fact, have been hidden by the seer or magician, who then proceeds to "find" them—the important point is that they should be found and social harmony restored until the next alert. Evil spirits are constantly on the lookout for opportunities to wreak havoc and a day will come when the village will once more call on the services of those who can restore calm and harmony to society. These techniques are cyclical in form: society is a perpetual renewing of Being through the endless cycle of life and death. For individuals, it is about being master of oneself and of one's speech, which acts as a kind of verbal mask behind which one can hide but which others must learn to decipher. To demonstrate one's self-control, it is important to know when to remain silent, as silence is the supreme reality. The Bambara believe that words, speech, and language only have value in terms of the silence that underlies them. They have a saying that says "Silence considers, while words refuse to think."

Given the photographs in this book and the apparent exuberance of the gestures and accompanying music, it may be difficult to believe that in sub-Saharan Africa, silence, not speech, is admired as the medicine capable of curing all ills. However, it is possible to be exuberant while not giving utterance to what is most important. It is clear that one can be influenced by a way of thinking and organizing human relations, even in one's own religion, while still remaining faithful to the languages and gestures of one's own community.

The African experience of ecstasy, illustrated in the photographs reproduced here, has a more apparent social character than Christian ecstasy. The phenomena referred to as possession do not happen by chance but, rather, generally coincide with events set by an unspoken timetable, such as periods of initiation, rites designed to bring the rains, and sessions of divination. The African experience of ecstasy opens a path to all believers to communicate with a world inaccessible to ordinary human senses.

Alongside the traditional religions often referred to as animist, Africa is home to every faith. The photographs clearly indicate that African religions have been, and continue to be, influenced by them. Syncretic movements and their particularities of attire and ornamentation, which were assumed to be the result of colonial influence, have in fact vastly increased since independence. Witchcraft has spread, as is always the case in times of crisis. Certain churches have specialized in fighting witchcraft. Others are less innocent than they may at first appear, but they take care to cloak their activities in secrecy.

The attire and postures of the worshippers pictured here reveal that Western society has had a profound impact on African thought and systems of organization. It is no longer an overwhelming destructive presence but a dialogue that, while still occasionally paroxysmal, is overall peaceful.

RITUAL SLAVERY

It is estimated that in Africa today there are some ten thousand girls and young women held in Vodun churches and convents, awaiting initiation. This is a modern form of ritual slavery: the girls are slaves not only of the gods, but also of the priests. They live in the church or convent until the end of their religious initiation period. They are often given or sold to the convent in expiation of an insult to the gods, sometimes reaching back several generations. They are held in seclusion until they attain the status of wives of the voduns. This generally takes several years, until the family finishes paying the costs of the initiation demanded by the priest. In times past, in times of war, women who placed themselves under the protection of a priest were free from persecution. In exchange, they had to accept initiation and serve the priest. Their lives were devoted to working in his fields, cleaning, cooking, and responding to his sexual needs.

Koumasi, Ghana

VODUN

Pierre Saulnier

The world of traditional African deities is a real challenge to explore given the large numbers of gods, their fluctuating identities and genealogies, their changing relations both with other gods and with humans depending on places and families, and their various functions. However, I will aim to do so, drawing on my experience in Porto-Novo and Adjohoun, in the province of Ouémé in Dahomey—now Benin—where I lived from 1962 to 1975 as a priest and Catholic missionary.

THE VISIBLE AND INVISIBLE WORLD

In Africa, there are two worlds, the visible and the invisible, which co-exist in symbiosis. Although the second world cannot be seen, it is, nonetheless, present in everyday life.

The invisible world encompasses God, who, while distant, is the basic principle behind existence and the origin of every characteristic of every individual. Each individual has his or her own $sê$[4], consisting of his or her own individual physical, moral, and intellectual characteristics.

The African pantheon also includes voduns, or lesser deities, which watch over natural elements such as rain, wind, fire, lightning, rainbows, fresh water and the ocean, the sun, the moon, day, and night. The ancestors of all men become vodun, and the aim of earthly existence is to become a vodun after a life on earth contributing to the community as much as possible. Vodun are also responsible for the virtues of plants and minerals.

Although little is known about it, the invisible world is present in every individual. As a Fon proverb has it, "Men's spit is white, but their blood is black."

THE ROLE OF THE ANCESTORS

Ancestors play a central role in African religions, including Vodun. Worshippers honor them to receive their bounty and avoid their anger, and to prevent their ghosts from returning to haunt their descendants.

Once the deceased has been buried, the family holds a wake lasting seven nights for a woman and nine for a man. The aim is to bring the family together around the deceased, remembering his or her life and enabling him or her to move on to the village of the ancestors. In Porto-Novo, seven nights after death for a woman, nine for a man, the deceased's skull was removed from the grave and washed. The skull is seen as the key to the individual's personality. The family sacrificed a cockerel for the skull and offered up prayers. The skull was then placed in a sack and hidden in a pot along with those of other recently deceased people, to be honored in a group ceremony. During this ceremony, each of the recently deceased was represented on the family altar devoted to the ancestors by an *asen* (a kind of small metal umbrella). At times other than funeral rites, it is still common to pour a little liquid on the ground before drinking as an offering to the ancestors.

VODUNS

Like the world, voduns possess a dual identity. They are ancestors raised to divinity, the deceased of each clan becoming gods as the generations pass. They are also forces of nature, for which each ancestor is held to be responsible.

Each vodun controls one natural element, internal or external. Sakpata is the god of smallpox, dysentery, skin diseases, and now AIDS. Gu is the god of metal, iron, and the forge, while So is the god of lightning. Dan is the vodun of beauty and wealth and is also the servant of God and the other vodun. The Hunve voduns are responsible for human fertility and sexuality in a social context. Legba is omnipresent as guardian not only of homes, but of markets and roads. He also represents protest and rebellion.

In the region of Porto-Novo and Ouémé, the renowned voduns Sakpata, Gu, and So are mythical Yoruba rulers whose descendants migrated from the east or the north. During the course of their migrations, these populations lost most of their original language, while retaining the memory of their origins. In Ouidah, the ancestral vodun is called Dangbe, (the royal python), while the Plas in the Grand-Popo region call their vodun Xu, (the sea). In Abomey, the royal faith worships the Nesuxue, ancestors of kings and princes. The vodun Dan, the serpent or rainbow, represents ancestors lost in the mists of time, whose names are no longer remembered. Dan symbolizes both male and female lineage.

In fact, these names are the generic terms for the gods, as every family has either its own Sakpata or So vodun, each with its own name. But, while there are a multitude of gods thanks to the great number of families, the amount of generic names for vodun are limited.

The name of the vodun Sakpata is generally not spoken, because it is too terrifying. Instead, people speak of Ayi (the earth) or Ayino (owner of the earth). These terms refer, first and foremost, to the earth as a physical space that, when cultivated, nourishes man. Secondly, it is a sociological space where men live together, united by the bonds of family, alliance, and neighborhood. Finally, it is a mythical space, because it is in this earth, in the family plot—perhaps, in the bedroom—that the dead are buried.

INSANITY AS BLESSING

For the Agni people of eastern Ivory Coast, mental instability is not a symptom of illness but rather a sign of mystic revelation. The gods of the air, the earth, water, and the forest choose their followers from among the mentally unstable. When a young woman suffers from hysteria or convulsive trances, she is taken to the school for fetish priestesses in Tanguelan. There, she spends four years studying with priestesses, who teach her to live with her *boson* (guardian angel). She must leave her former life behind and devote herself to her *boson*, whom she marries at her initiation. Every day, she must follow a strict set of rituals, which include getting up at four in the morning to clean herself with the bark of the magical ravia tree (her skin must never touch water) She is not allowed to look at herself in a mirror or see her family, and she must be absolutely chaste, forgoing all sexual contact, even with her husband.

Tanguelan, Ivory Coast

Thus, while the dead no longer walk among their families, they are still present and may even make their presence felt. That is why the land belongs to a community rather than to an individual. It is inalienable. The local chief can make a temporary loan of the land but cannot grant ownership of it. Ancestors are not for sale.

The serious social problems facing many African countries today are in part due to the negligence of this fundamental law of African life.

TWINS AND *ABIKUS*

Twin and triplet births are another example of the sudden intrusion of the invisible into the visible world. Twins and triplets are given special names and are the object of particular rites. They must be treated equally all their lives. If one of them should die, the mother or the surviving twin should carry a small carving representing the deceased.

Death itself is present in life in *abikus* (children born after the death of at least two brothers or sisters). It is believed that the dead siblings return to their mother's womb. They are commonly given the name of an object, animal, or something meaningless, so that Death does not recognize them as a human being.

VODUN WORSHIP

No other form of religious worship appears to be organized like that of Vodun. It is characterized by a fairly long period of initiation. Men and women are initiated into the religion after being chosen from within their family to replace the deceased or to fulfill a vow made after a cure or a birth.

As soon as the initiation begins, the person goes through a ritual of death and resurrection, losing his or her identity so as to take on that of the deity, of whom the person becomes the vodun-*si*, or wife. (*Si* means "wife," in Fon.) The new initiate is consecrated to the deity, taking on a new name as a sign of a new identity. The initiate's role is to make the vodun's presence felt in the community, through periods of possession and trance, miming actions, and by the initiate's whole being. The initiate becomes the vodun, even outside of any religious context. Showing disrespect to the vodun-si—and, therefore, to the vodun—through insults, beatings, or calling the initiate by his or her former name is an act of sacrilege and desecration. Anyone guilty of such an offence must make up for the insult by paying for and organizing a ceremony of re-consecration.

Vodun worship is led by a vodun-*no* (owner of the vodun, in Fon), under the authority of the head of the family. Sacrifices are a major part of the ceremony, with the vodun-si drinking the blood of the sacrificed animals, as a

The invisible world of vodun, ancestors, and God is constantly present in the visible world of humans. When a child is born, the family wants to know which ancestor led to the birth and the identity of the child. If there are no clear signs of the child's ancestral identity, the family will consult a soothsayer and healer, or specialist in the art of Fa divination, as a conduit between the world beyond and the present. Fa divination consists of eight cowry shells attached to a bracelet, thrown onto a bed of white powder. The shells leave marks forming one of 156 possible signs that the diviner interprets with proverbs and myths.

Later, when a child reaches adulthood, Fa divination is used to reveal his or her *se*, or fate. Divination is used to decide on a proposed marriage or to discover the causes of ill luck, such as a failed project, illness, or death. Such ill fortune can be caused by an *aze-to* (father of witchcraft), a witch, or some ill-judged action that has aroused the wrath of the ancestors. People who have been hit by lightning, or who die of smallpox or in traffic accidents, for example, are believed to have been struck down respectively by So, Sakpata, and Gu. The earthly representatives of each of these vodun must then take over the deceased person's body and possessions, returning them to the family only upon payment of a large fine and costly sacrifices. The rites associated with the *To-xosus* (kings of the water, in Fon) are another example of vodun worship. These relate to children born with disabilities or physical deformities. They were cast into the water, their natural element, at birth.

Vodun uses many plants, for their beneficial properties. Each deity is associated with a particular plant, whose qualities were discovered and have been handed down by the ancestors. The healer chants incantations over the plants to direct their powers where needed, warding off evil or calling down a benefit.

CHRISTIANITY AND SYNCRETISM

This rapid overview might seem to give a rather idealized vision of Vodun prior to colonization in the late nineteenth century. There is no doubt that it remains a living religion, with ceremonies remaining unchanged for decades. However, it should be noted that this vision of the world and the relationship between its visible and invisible dimensions does have its own limits and carries within itself its own seeds of rebellion. The vodun Legba, for example, opposes overly strict order, sowing discord and panic among the gods. Voduns fight and die. Texts record the murder of the vodun Dan, whose divinity was stripped from him and his power stolen by placing the decapitated head of the serpent in a calabash placed on a vodun-si's head.

THE POWER OF WOMEN IS FEARED

The school for fetish priestesses in Tanguelan is led by a female initiate known by the title of *comian* (oracle) of the Agni people. She is chosen by the Agni gods at the funeral of the former *comian* from among two hundred candidates, her name spoken by a woman in a trance. Only women can study at this school. In Ivory Coast, as in most countries in sub-Saharan Africa, society is matriarchal, with filiation passing down the female line. Women are, thus, powerful and feared.

Tanguelan, Ivory Coast

It can also be very difficult to find new initiates. Often only women can be found in the initiatory shrines, with their menfolk in opposition. In other instances, parents seek to protect their children from being chosen as initiates by baptizing them at birth or entrusting them to Christian missionaries just before they are due to be handed over to the initiatory shrine. Such actions can be problematic, because other members of the family may not approve of this decision. Yet Christianity seems both to free people from fear and the constraints of their social and religious duties and to provide them with an alternative vision of relations, both with the invisible world and with other men and women.

Today, traditional forms of worship tend to be confined to outlying rural districts. Families who have moved to the towns and cities refuse to consecrate their children, although this does not prevent them from making gifts of money or taking part in ceremonies. Some observe both Christian and Vodun beliefs. It is quite common to find a chicken or goat to be sacrificed by a soothsayer or healer in the trunk of a car taking a family to Sunday mass.

New religious groups blend aspects of Christianity and Vodun in their services and their religious doctrine. For example, the "Ijo-Fa" doctrine of the Church of Fa, founded in 1943, is based on the trinity of God, Ifa, and Jesus, with Jesus being Ifa's grandfather. Many of the photographs in this book contain Christian crosses for this reason.

Vodun has, thus, undergone both internal and external changes. Some of the photographs show Westerners undergoing initiation rites. This seems to be an ever more frequent occurrence, as does calling on the services of *marabouts* (witch doctors). What do such worshippers hope to find in trances of possession and animal sacrifices? Although a foreigner may be able to reach a full understanding of the African vision of the universe, how can he enter this world and even be consecrated, given that the world of voduns was originally based on a microcosm of the family, with its own values, expectations, and limits?

African slaves took their deities with them to Bahia in Brazil, where they are known as *candomble*, a Yoruba word. In Haiti, they are known as voodoo. When it left Africa, vodun worship lost its ancestral aspect and its bond with the earth. It was no longer a family heritage, although some aspects were maintained, such as the control of natural elements, conflicts, and private and social tensions. These were widened to include the whole community, with no regard to origin. Individuals were faced with a wider range of possibilities. The festive, enthusiastic, warm, even exuberant dimensions of vodun worship were maintained and took on greater importance. This is found even in Catholic churches in the Western world, when African choirs are invited to

sing at services. This corresponds to a natural need to unite body and spirit, dance and song, in prayer, to demonstrate one's emotions and feelings, and to leave the difficulties of daily life behind for a short while.

In Vodun, in its various syncretic offshoots, and even in official Christian churches, people come to worship to express the same needs and difficulties: illness, failure, death, and so on. They attribute these ills to an evil spirit, a witch that they must protect themselves against, or to a devil that must be exorcised.

Vodun is controversial, but the traditional modes of thinking that attribute all failure to an external agent, whether another person, a dead relative, or a god, are the same in other religions. Vodun worshippers hope to find the same good fortune or success, but by making their faith in the invisible world subject to it, they risk losing their relationship with it and reducing Vodun to a utilitarian means of controlling the forces of nature.

A MASKED HEALER

This healer carefully protects his true identity, which has made him a local legend; no-one has ever seen his face. He treats people by consulting an oracle, because according to African tradition, illness has a supernatural cause.

According to traditional beliefs, humans have one body and two souls. The vital soul controls the body, while the free soul leaves the body to roam, particularly at night when the body is asleep. The free soul is unstable and, therefore, vulnerable, and illness occurs when the body and the two souls are out of harmony. Lying, theft, adultery, jealousy, and anything that harms other people damage the vital soul, while evil spells and black magic threaten the free soul when it wanders at night. The healer, thus, treats the souls in order to cure the body.

In Africa, illness also has a social aspect, involving not only the victim but also his or her relations and community. The victim must be cured before the disease—caused by personal faults—spreads to others. In the past, for this reason, the king's health was vital to the well-being of his people. When he fell ill, he was executed to protect his people from harm. A good king was a king in good health.

Ivory Coast

CHASTE MAGICIANS

This magician from Ivory Coast must abstain from sexual intercourse prior to each ceremony or else he will lose his magical powers. He must concentrate in order to channel the magical forces found in plants, trees, and animals. After channeling these forces, usually in the depths of night, he locks them into objects such as wooden dolls, pots, animal horns, or bottles. When someone calls on his services—to become pregnant, to pass an examination, or to sign a contract, for example—the magician reactivates the charms by sprinkling them with the blood of an animal sacrifice. To make their charms more potent, some magicians go so far as to sacrifice children. Some years ago, customs officers in Togo intercepted a suitcase full of the heads of recently decapitated children intended as charms for students hoping to pass their university exams.

On another occasion, during a presidential election in Benin, one of the candidates, Nicéphore Soglo, repeatedly fell ill. No explanation could be found for his illnesses and he was transferred to a military hospital in France, where the puzzled French doctors eventually called on a Beninese magician to help discover the cause of his illness. It was a case of gas gangrene, believed to have been caused by an old women by means of a *shakatu* (magic cannon), a sort of tube filled with various products that is used to cast spells from a distance. To make the *shakatu*, the old woman would have needed to make physical contact with the candidate, perhaps by shaking his hand, to acquire something as little as a drop of sweat to make the charm. Nicéphore Soglo was later elected president of Benin, and took to wearing gloves to shake hands in public.

Abengourou, Ivory Coast

THE INITIATES' SACRED DANCE

When the novices' mystical seclusion comes to an end, the vodun-si come from all over the region for a week-long celebration marking the end of their time in a Vodun convent. Their families observe the occasion with a display of wealth and prestige, and compete to perform the best sacred dance. On the final day, after purifying themselves in the forest, the novices dance and shout in the main village square. They go round the square seven times then sit, balancing on earthen jugs. If the jug breaks, the novice is guilty of bad behavior and is disgraced. If the jug remains whole, their entry into the great Vodun religious fellowship is celebrated with dancing. Each novice performs a dance in which she changes her cloth wrap nearly forty times, dancing for three or four minutes between each change.

Vogan region, Togo

ASHANTIS FORCED THEIR ENEMIES TO WALK BAREFOOT

When the Ashantehene, or king of the Ashanti, dies, the priests process through the streets of Kumasi wailing in grief to demonstrate their allegiance to the king and his sacred golden stool. The golden stool is extremely important to the Ashanti. They believe this is where their soul and the king's power resides. If their bare feet or buttocks touch the ground, they are defiled and disaster will befall their family. In times gone by, they merely had to remove their enemies' footwear and place their bare feet on the ground to destroy them utterly.

Kumasi, Ghana

31

FOLLOWERS OF THE HIGH PRIEST
OF THE SACRED FOREST

This photograph was taken some twenty-five years ago, on the occasion of the death of the high priest of the sacred forest of Be, in Lome, the capital of Togo. These women are followers of the priest's vodun. Some of the women lived with him in the forest as recluses. Over several days, they paid homage to him before the final separation. When the next priest is appointed, the women will meet again in the same place, wearing the same clothes. However, since then, for the past quarter of a century, no priest has come forward to take on this highly prestigious role. It is one of the most important in the Vodun hierarchy in Togo, but the high priest must live confined to the sacred forest, with no modern amenities of any kind.

Sacred forest of Be, Lome, Togo

STRICT CODES OF CONDUCT

The Zion Christian Church is renowned for the strict rules it imposes on its worshippers, who are not allowed to drink alcohol, smoke, or eat pork. The church also preaches sexual abstinence, based on a belief that sex turns men away from God by diminishing their devotion to prayer. Zionist Christians believe in nonviolence, yet the men wear an army-style khaki uniform to put them in the frame of mind to defend their religion.

Moria, South Africa

ZIONIST CHRISTIAN WOMEN

The Zion Christian Church is the biggest religious organization among black South Africans. It is an independent church, with more than four million worshippers and nearly four thousand parishes. The Zionist Christian faith is a blend of Christian doctrine and African beliefs. Its followers believe in miracle cures and ancestor worship.

Every year at Easter, more than a million Zionist Christians gather together in Zion City Moria, north of Pretoria, in one of the biggest religious celebrations anywhere in Africa. For four days, the worshippers pray, the men on one side and women on the other. Zionist Christians believe that men were created in God's image to serve Him, while women were created to serve men and satisfy his desires.

Moria, South Africa

THE GOD SANPONNA PROTECTS
AGAINST EPIDEMICS

This young man is an initiate in the Yoruba faith in southern Nigeria. This religion is similar to the form of Vodun practiced in neighboring Togo and Benin. It is an initiatory—in other words, secret—faith that defines men by their relationship with the gods who rule the world. To serve the gods, worshippers must learn a secret language and rituals in an initiation period that generally lasts several years. This young man is in the service of the god Sanponna (also known as Sakpata in certain Vodun faiths), who was formerly the god of smallpox. Sanponna, one of the most powerful gods in the Yoruba pantheon, protects men against epidemics. The white marks represent the scars left by the disease after it was conquered by Sanponna. As the Yoruba faith is shrouded in secrecy, it is hard to obtain explanations for the black and white paint on the man's body. One theory says it represents the combat between Sanponna and a god from another religion. Today, Sanponna is believed to protect men from modern epidemics, including AIDS.

Ibadan, Nigeria

A "PENIS SHRINKER"

To protect this man from a lynching at the hands of a mob in the central marketplace in Lome, the Togo police took him into custody. His crime was to be a Hausa from Nigeria. It is dangerous to be foreign and a Muslim in Lome, where fear of "penis shrinkers" haunts the populace. In African societies, the penis represents power and wealth; any erectile dysfunction, no matter how fleeting, is a cause for dishonor. Since the nineteenth century, in periods of economic crisis, rumors of penis shrinking have regularly swept through towns and cities in sub-Saharan Africa, with often devastating results.

This man's mistake was to shake a trader's hand, who immediately began to scream that he could feel his penis shrinking. The Nigerian was chased by an angry mob who, by the time the police arrived, had covered him in gas and threatened to burn him alive.

Lome, Togo

PRAYING FOR A CURE

In the 1980s, when AIDS first struck central Africa, the people of Congo called the disease "the imaginary syndrome to discourage lovers." It was years before they accepted that the disease was real—and deadly. Faced with this scourge, many Africans turned to God in the hope of a cure. Many evangelical African churches specialize in so-called "miracle cures," allowing their priests and prophets, in just a few short years, to make a fortune. AIDS continues to ravage the population, and central Africa remains the worst afflicted area in the entire world.

Congo

PRIEST IN A MYSTIC COMA

Bwiti is a syncretic religion, taking elements from the ancestor worship of the Fang of Gabon and from Christian influences dating from French colonization. Paradoxically, this is a way to survive the influx of the major world religions of Christianity and Islam, whose presence is increasingly felt across Africa. Bwiti rituals are based on the sacred plant iboga, which has a hallucinogenic effect. This Bwiti priest has just eaten a large amount of iboga as a means of contacting his ancestors. The worshippers believe that his soul has left his body to journey in the realm of the dead. Under the influence of the drug, he remains sitting in a comatose state, incapable of movement. Sometimes, worshippers overdose on iboga during these initiation rituals, and they end up hospitalized or dead.

Gabon

IN THE LAND OF THE DEAD

Followers of the Bwiti religion believe that the dead live in a parallel world, close to that of the living, and that dead ancestors help the living to solve their problems. To speak to them, believers need to eat iboga, considered a sacred plant, and which contains ibogaine, a powerful psychotropic drug. (In the United States and the Netherlands, ibogaine is used as a substitute drug for heroin addicts.) Legend recounts how God once surprised a pygmy when he was up in a tree, picking fruit. The pygmy fell from the tree and died. God gathered up his spirit then cut off his fingers and toes to plant them in the forest. Ever since, iboga plants have grown in these places.

Gabon

THE IBIDIO PRIEST REMAINS
IN THE VILLAGE

In Ibidio villages in the Niger delta in Nigeria, the oldest male inhabitant from a line of ritual priests is guardian of customs and of the gods. He holds the symbols of his sacred powers: a lance to hunt evil spirits and an elephant tusk to represent his sacred power. Tradition forbids him from leaving his village, on pain of death.

Agbaja, Nigeria

MASKS ARE DANGEROUS

I came across this Yoruba mask in the streets of Lagos. Before being allowed to take this photograph, I had to barter and pay a small sum to placate the god in the mask. To this day, someone taking a photograph of such a mask without permission takes his life into his hands. As with many African rituals, the god's secrets are never revealed to the uninitiated, and the precise meaning of the scene and the mask remain a mystery.

Lagos, Nigeria

THE POWER OF ELEPHANT TUSKS

Priest-kings are often members of secret societies such as the society of the leopard, whose members wear necklaces of leopard fangs. This Oguta priest-king is holding an elephant tusk to symbolize his power. Nigeria is still home to two types of secret societies. The first, linked with witch-craft, aims to harm. Its members go out at night in masks to kill people they accuse of theft or adultery, or simply who are their enemies. In times gone by, members of the leopard society killed their victims with iron claws shaped like those of a leopard. These days, they prefer poison. The second type of secret society, of which this priest is a member, aims to protect men against witchcraft and harmful spells, and plays a role in maintaining social order.

Oguta, Nigeria

SOOTHSAYERS CAN SEE THE SPIRITS OF THE DEAD

In Imo state, Nigeria, the *idiong*—usually a hereditary role—is both a seer and a kind of psychologist. He is consulted for various issues, ranging from the loss of property or problems with relationships, to infertility, incurable illness, or unexplained deaths. In villages in southern Nigeria his role is to help and to cure, but his formidable magical powers can be intimidating. He seeks guidance from spirits, using bells to summon them and covering his eyes with a white powder which allows him to see into the spirit world; this omniscience makes him as feared as he is respected.

Aboh region, Nigeria

FEAR OF MAGIC

The *Eze Izombe* in the village of Amakpu, in Imo State in Nigeria, is nearly 80 years old. He once had extraordinary magical powers, passed down to him from his father, in which everything he said or wished would come true. His magical sight could reveal thieves and punish them by casting a spell. However, since he converted to Catholicism, his magic powers have vanished. Three years ago, he was invited to visit the bishop of Owerri. When he was presented to the bishop in his magical garb with his eyes made up, the bishop believed that he was a witch come to cast a spell on him, and he was thrown out of the bishop's residence. Ever since, he has avoided scaring the other members of his parish, by removing his makeup and red attire to go to Sunday mass.

Amakpu, Imo State, Nigeria

TO SEE MEANS TO KNOW

This priest from Imo State in Nigeria is surrounded by photographs of the Nigerian president and of military leaders he has met. The photographs symbolize his power and social standing. The same is true for the photograph of banknotes on his right, which represent wealth and power—a wealthy priest is a powerful man. The priest's red attire symbolizes his ability to transform himself and go over to the other side—the world of night, while the white makeup around his eyes indicates that he can "see" in the invisible world. (Seeing in this context does not mean looking, but knowing.) Those who can see in the invisible world know everything that happens in the real world, whether the village, the province, or even the country.

Imo State, Nigeria

THE PUNISHMENT FOR INSULTING GOD IS DEATH

As with most practitioners of African religions, the Igbo of southeastern Nigeria worship one supreme god, Ala. However, Ala is only rarely represented in shrines. More commonly represented is Amadi Oha, the god of the skies, and lord of thunder and lightning, who oversees the cycle of life from birth to death. The priest's machete is used to prepare food but also to kill anyone who threatens to offend the god.

Uzuakoli, Nigeria

THE SACRED STATUE OF OHAFIA

In the Owerri region of southeastern Nigeria, *mbaris*, also known as *obus*, are shrines devoted to ancestor worship. Tradition dictates that each clan has its own *mbari*, where the priest prepares traditional medicines to cure all sorts of ailments.

Local scholars believe this shrine to be two hundred years old. The statues represent the founder of the community, a highly reputed healer, who was attacked by another clan and had to flee across the marshes with his servants, carrying his wife on his shoulders. The sculpture at the center recreates this episode. The shrine is now used for meetings of the village's secret society. The healer's relics, kept inside the shrine, protect pilgrims from disease. Twins and menstruating women are forbidden from entering the shrine, and no black clothes are allowed inside either. Very few *mbari* shrines are left in the region. Most have been destroyed, and the statues stolen. To prevent Ohafia's statues from being stolen, village elders stand guard day and night.

Ohafia, Nigeria

THE SOUL OF THE DECEASED
FLOATS OVERHEAD

Among the Igbo of Nigeria, a head made of carved wood, as worn on the top of this man's skull, represents the head of a recently decapitated enemy. (Years ago, the actual head would have been exhibited.) The soul of the deceased, as represented by the sculpture, is thought to float over the head of the wearer. The taboos of the ancestral faith dictate that no part of the mask-wearer's body should be visible. The mask's guardians do, however, allow a man or woman who has produced an infant to see part of the masked man's body.

Umuahia, Nigeria

THIS SKULL HAS A SOUL

This crest was made around the end of the nineteenth century from the head of a captured enemy fighter. It contains the soldier's vital energies and protects its wearer from witches. To prevent the soul from straying, the skull's guardian feeds it with regular offerings and sacrifices. The priest asks the ancestors for permission to exhibit it. Once it has been granted, he can carry out a number of magic rituals. The skull's wearer must be pure, which means having avoided sexual contact in the days immediately before putting it on. When the rituals have been completed, the skull is placed back in its box in the home of the oldest male inhabitant.

Nigeria

A WITCH-CHILD IN KINSHASA

Pierre, aged 12, is hiding behind a homemade mask. His uncle threw him out of his home, accusing him of having killed his grandmother with a spell. Pierre is just one of thousands of children accused of witchcraft and abandoned on the streets of Kinshasa, capital of the Democratic Republic of Congo. Seventy percent of cases of abandoned children are due to accusations of witchcraft. Preachers at the new evangelical churches springing up all over the DRC accuse the children of being demons in the service of evil and claim the devil hides in their eyes. The populace is terrified of these "possessed" children. Many are mistreated, beaten, and tortured by their parents or by exorcists, who drive the devil from the childrens' bodies by starving and whipping them. These priests claim that the children must suffer to give themselves over to God and be delivered from evil.

Kinshasa, Democratic Republic of Congo

SHANGO, GOD OF LIGHTNING

For the Edo of Nigeria, religion is a major part of everyday life and priests are powerful figures that inspire fear. They are paid for every ritual they carry out. I had to pay to take this photograph in the shrine of the most important Shango priest in the Edo kingdom, or face the wrath of the god. In Edo mythology, Shango is the god of thunder and lightning. He is virile, violent, and pitiless, punishing liars, thieves, and murderers by striking them down with lightning. The Edo believe that a home struck by lightning during a storm is a punishment by the gods and that the owners must atone for their sins by making the priest an offering of a ram and some alcohol. In his shrine, the priest is surrounded by statues of his ancestors, who watch over him and protect him as long as he honors them with sacrifices and offerings of fruit. When the priest dies, the statues and other objects used in his rituals are destroyed. The shrine stands empty until the priest's soul returns in reincarnated form.

Benin City, Nigeria

MESSENGER OF THE GODS

In her shrine in what was formerly known as Bendel State in Nigeria, the Edo priestess watches over the spirits of the ancestors and the gods. She knows them, speaks to them, and serves them. She is the sole link between the world of gods and the world of men, receiving offerings, offering up prayers, and making intercessions on behalf of worshippers. When the gods have a message for the faithful, the priestess becomes their mouthpiece. She is sacred and must submit to the whims of the gods, who sometimes forbid her to have sexual intercourse or to eat certain types of fruit or meat. If she follows these rules, she is granted magical powers in the form of *jujus* (fetishes), which are similar in function to magic wands in the Western tradition. Originally, *jujus* were little dolls with magical powers. (The word comes from the French *joujou*, a diminutive of *jouet*, which means toy.) The power of the *juju* is feared throughout Nigeria and the Gulf of Benin.

Benin City, Nigeria

THE SACRED LANGUAGES OF THE VODUN

Two young novices in a Vodun convent flank the vodun-si in charge of their education. Every member of a Vodun society undergoes religious training during a period of seclusion in a convent, which can last from three lunar months to three years, although these days the initiation period is generally shortened to two weeks to allow the children to go to school. In general, large families try to send at least one son or daughter to a convent to receive the protection of a vodun and to avoid the depredations of evil spirits who bring illness and poverty. During their initiation period, the novices learn to serve a particular vodun and to speak the deity's own particular sacred language, one which is incomprehensible to the uninitiated. The novice may only speak this language throughout the period of initiation.

Mono, Benin

EYOS ARE GUARDIANS OF THE SOUL

Eyos are the guardians of the orishas (vodun deities) of the
king of Lagos and of the souls of men. They wear masks
and take part in an annual festival in the streets of Nigeria's
biggest city. Some hide beneath their white robes a bag
containing *jujus*, magical objects that punish anyone who
disrupts worship of the orisha*s* that they protect. In the
Orisha religion, it is believed that men have two souls: the
first is their vital soul, which belongs to them and gives life
to their body. The second is a free soul, which is transient
and is lent to them for their lifetime. When they die, this
second soul returns to the ocean, where it joins the souls of
all the dead waiting to be reincarnated. Contrary to Buddhist
interpretation of reincarnation, in this part of Africa, souls
are believed to have free will. They choose their own life and
can decide to be reincarnated as rich and healthy or as poor
and sick. Many souls choose to be poor because they are
under the influence of evil spirits that lead them astray.

Ikeja neighborhood, Lagos, Nigeria

THE ORISHA OF NIGERIA

These two young girls in southern Nigeria are shortly to be initiated into the Yoruba Orisha religion. As soon as they were born, their parents consulted a *babalawo* (soothsayer) to find out which orisha they should serve. When they become adults, they may serve several gods from the hundreds of the Yoruba pantheon. Some orishas are very popular, such as Shango, the god of thunder and lightning; Orunmila, goddess of divination and fate; Eshu, messenger of the supreme God; and Ogun, god of war and iron.

Nigeria

THE SPIRITUAL SON OF THE GOD OF LIGHTNING

This child is thought to be the spiritual son of Hevieso, Vodun god of thunder and lightning. He is sacred because he was born to an infertile woman cured by the deity, and his whole life has been dictated by this religious context. His parents have always taken him with them to Vodun ceremonies, where he has watched the dancing, trances, sacrifices, and prayers that mark the Vodun religious calendar. During one such ceremony, he fell into a trance to the sound of a drum, a clear sign that he was ready for initiation. He was then "kidnapped" and held in this Vodun convent devoted to Hevieso for the period of initiation. No one may comb or cut his hair before the end of this period.

   Children are sometimes chosen by Vodun priests during ceremonies to be taken to a convent. If the parents object, the priest threatens them with serious ailments or ill fortune, until they agree to obey his sacred decision. People whose crops or homes have been struck by lightning must send their children to serve Hevieso or else fall prey to insanity or paralysis.

Benin

RITUAL VODUN EQUIPMENT

Plastic dolls and soft toys are used in Vodun rites for the goddess Mami Wata in countries throughout the Gulf of Benin. Such equipment began to be used in the mid-twentieth century, along with the prints from India of Vishnu, Rama, and other Hindu deities that flooded the African market at around the same time. These images became associated with the prosperity of the Indian merchants who sold them and so worshippers began making wooden or cement statuettes of Hindu deities to decorate shrines to Mami Wata, goddess of the ocean, prosperity, and beauty. To this day, worshippers decorate their shrines with imported toys as symbols of prosperity, believing that goods imported from abroad are inherently beautiful.

Togo

SIXTEEN IS A SACRED NUMBER

This Nigerian Orisha priestess is in the service of Shango, the god of thunder and lightning. Orisha is a close cousin of the Vodun religions of Benin and Togo. The Yoruba refer to their Vodun deities as orishas, and they fulfil the same functions as vodun in Benin, protecting or punishing humans, and acting as intermediaries between men and the sole all-powerful God. The Fon of Benin call this supreme god Mawo, while the Yoruba call him Olorun or Olodumare. The Yoruba creation myth recounts how God asked Oduduwa to create the earth in the holy city of Ife. Later, sixteen other orishas created men and life on earth. The Yoruba pantheon consists of the descendants of these sixteen gods, with almost a thousand deities in all. Sixteen is, therefore, a sacred number for the Yoruba.

Nigeria

DEATH OF A KING

The Ashantehene King Nana Opoku Ware II has just died. This man, covered in white, has been in a trance for eight hours and is part of one of the many delegations who have come to pay their last respects to the king. On his head he is wearing the fetishes that will protect the dead king from the witches who will attempt to interrupt the ceremony and the king's journey to the realm of ancestors. An Ashanti king's funeral is an event of great importance. In times past, when the Ashantehene died, his wives and a hundred or so servants followed him to the grave to serve him in the after-life and the royal executioners scoured the streets of his capital, Kumasi, killing anyone they found to provide the king with company in the other world.

Kumasi, Ghana

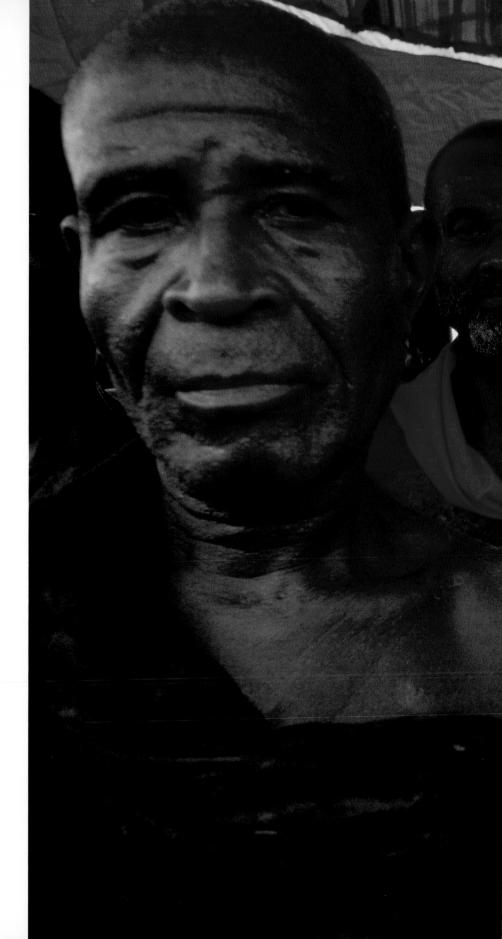

ATTRACTING AGNI GODS

The dancers of Tanguelan sprinkle their bodies with kaolin in order to attract the gods, who sit astride them, taking possession of their bodies and spirits. The dancers go into a trance, and leave behind their human state to become incarnations of the gods.

Tanguelan, Ivory Coast

71

GAMBADA, A VERY VIOLENT DEITY

Gambada, the vodun of iron, is extremely violent, and has just left this man's body during a ceremony. The man he "rides" (whose body he enters during a trance) is uncontrollable and insensitive to pain. He jumps constantly and bangs his head against the floor, or walks on shards of glass, apparently without pain, to show the congregation that he is powerful and fearless. Gambada is a terrifying figure, and it takes at least three people to prevent the man whose body he has entered from being seriously injured. Once Gambada's violence is spent, he leaves the man, who collapses and remains unconscious for a few minutes before coming to his senses. When he awakes, he does not remember anything of the episode.

Anfouin, Togo

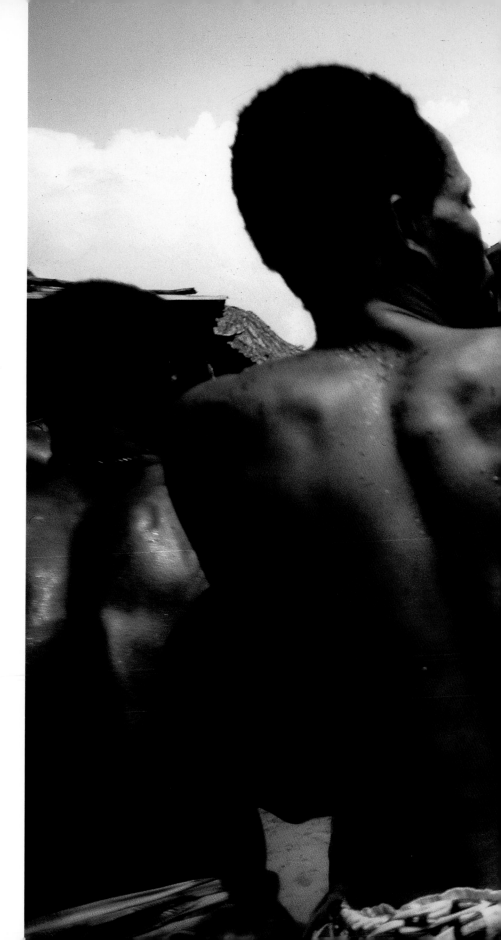

THE PRIEST MAKES THE SUN TURN

In Togo, in the sacred forest of Lome, surrounded by his vodun-si, this priest is dancing by imitating the wings of a bird preparing for flight, and is said to be making the sun turn. In West African languages of the Ewe family, the verb "to dance" literally means "to make the sun turn." Physical expression plays a key role in Vodun ceremonies: gestures, movements, and poses all invite the deities to celebrate and restore harmony between man and nature. The Ewe of southern Togo dance to mark births, marriages, initiations, and burials. Dancing creates a feeling of physical and spiritual wellbeing, and is the most complete expression of piety and prayer.

Sacred forest of Be, Lome, Togo

75

YOUNG INITIATES ARE NOT PERMITTED TO SPEAK

Vodun is one of the most widespread of African religions. The rituals and names of the gods change from country to country, but their function remains the same. This priest serves the goddess of water and the ocean, known as Mami Wata or Yemanja. It is unusual for men to serve this goddess but, in Togo and Benin, where this faith is particularly widespread, men are permitted to, according to local necessity. The two young girls undergoing initiation—one of them just six years old—will remain as recluses in the convent for two years. They will not be allowed to leave or to speak to strangers before they have learned how to serve Mami Wata well. They must learn her secret language and all the rituals of her worship. For example, the goddess only likes ram, duck, and fresh food made with white corn, oil, onion, and salt. She will only allow white and blue attire, which reminds her of the water of the river that is her home. Today, fewer and fewer girls are being initiated in Vodun convents, as the period of seclusion is thought to be too long.

Aneho convent, Togo

SLAVES OF THE GODS

These young girls are about to join a Vodun convent, where they will spend seven days cut off from their families and the rest of the world. They will learn sacred songs and dances, prayers, and the initiatory languages and rituals associated with the convent's vodun. During this period they are forbidden from running, playing, shouting, or arguing, from turning their backs to a full initiate, or from uncovering their heads. They will become slaves to the deity and submit wholly to the authority of the *midawo* (high priest), who will teach them the secrets of the convent's own religious practices. On the eighth day, their hair will be shaved off, and they will change their cloth wraps three times a day. In the morning, they will wear red wraps to symbolize the sunrise. In the afternoon, their wraps will be deep blue, the color of the sky. In the evening, they will wear white, the color of purity. After this time they will spend anywhere from twenty days to three months studying before taking an examination. In times gone by, the test was very strict. Novices gave their answers kneeling, with their arms crossed, and if they answered incorrectly, the priest beat them or made them kneel on broken palm nut shells. These days, the punishments are less harsh. Once the test is over, the children will become vodun-si and will be allowed to return to their families.

Benin

SACRED SLAVES

Initiation into the Vodun faith is expensive, and these novices' parents have not yet managed to pay the sum demanded by the priest. They must therefore leave their daughters in the convent until they have repaid their debt. The girls are entirely at the priest's mercy and must tend his land, cook, clean, and wash his clothes. Many are subject to sexual abuse. There are estimated to be over twelve thousand sacred slaves in the Gulf of Benin.

MAHOUNON, PRINCESS OF THE UNIVERSE

This twenty-two-year-old priestess is unmarried and lives as a recluse in her convent in Ouidah. In theory, there are no spiritual authorities in the Vodun religion. However, for many believers, the Princess of the Universe, known as Mahounon, is one of the highest Vodun dignitaries in Benin. She answers only to Mawu, the invisible, sexless supreme being, who is beyond the reach of men. The supreme Vodun god's name comes from *ma*, meaning "do not," and *wu*, meaning "kill." Mawu is the god who does not let men die, providing them with the food, drink, and clothes they need. The various ethnic groups in Benin trust their God implicitly. However, he is too busy to deal directly with human affairs, which he entrusts to voduns, his messengers on earth. These capricious deities are feared for the punishments they mete out to those who fail to honor them. Worshippers must placate the gods with gifts and sacrifices.

Ouidah, Benin

ALA-WE.

AHOYO

THE DAHO KPASSENON
AND THE IROKO TREE

According to local beliefs, whoever sees Daho Kpassenon's eyes will become blind, but the legend is all that remains today. Despite his headgear, all the inhabitants of the town of Ouidah, in Benin, have seen the face of the Daho Kpassenon, leader of the royal Vodun religion and keeper of Ouidah's sacred forest.

The forest owes its sacred nature to King Kpasse, founder of the kingdom of Ouidah, who is believed to have died in the forest and been transformed into an iroko tree; the tree is now sacred to the Vodun religion in Ouidah. Nonbelievers are not permitted to enter the forest. When a retired captain in the French army broke the taboo by building a house in the forest he was harassed by nightmares, waking visions, and evil spirits until he fled.

Worshippers of the iroko tree scarify and tattoo their faces. When they die, they are buried in the forest, their heads turned towards the ocean. After five years, the Daho Kpassenon and members of the deceased's family exhume the head and decorate it with the family's finest jewels.

Ouidah, Benin

THE AMAZONS OF ABOMEY

The Amazon leader is flanked by two dignitaries. He is the sole remaining man in this army of warrior women, which now plays only a religious role in modern-day Benin. The Amazon army was founded by King Agadja (1708–1740). His father, King Houegbadja, had founded a corps of female elephant hunters, who also acted as bodyguards; Agadja turned the women into real warriors. Some women joined of their own free will, while others were enrolled forcibly after their husbands complained to the king that they were difficult to live with. Military service taught them discipline, and military life gave them an outlet to express their character. They protected the king on the battlefield and took active part in combat, devoting their entire lives to warfare; they were not allowed to marry or to have children. This army of women, often drunk on gin, hardened to suffering and prepared to give up their lives, proved doughty warriors, leading the male troops into battle and urging them on. A little over a century ago, when France was fighting the kingdom of Abomey, over four thousand Amazon soldiers took the field.

Abomey, Benin

WORSHIPPING THE PYTHON

In this priest's shrine, a great celebration is held every seven years for worshippers of the python. During the celebration, forty-one young virgins fetch sacred water, which they pour into a large jar for purification ceremonies. Today, when a royal python dies, it is buried in the shrine in Ouidah and honored with the same funeral rites as men. Rather than saying "the Python is dead," worshippers say "night has fallen."

Python worship dates back three hundred years, to just after the fratricidal war between the kingdoms of Abomey and Houedas (now called Ouidah). After the defeat of the Houedas, their king, Kpasse, sought refuge in a great forest to escape the warriors of King Ghezo of Abomey. Pythons emerged from the forest to chase his pursuers, and Kpasse was saved. In gratitude, he built three huts in the forest and began worshipping the pythons, a tradition which continues to the present day. The deity's altar is in the largest of the three huts and is used for invocations and prayers. The other two huts are used for purification and exorcism ceremonies.

Ouidah python shrine, Benin

TWIN RITUAL AND THE GODDESS MAMI WATA

Every day, this young girl prays to the spirit of dead twins while stroking the statuettes that represent them. Twins are celebrated in special rituals throughout the Gulf of Guinea. In the Vodun religion, their birth is seen as a blessing from the gods. If one of the twins dies, their mother—or a sister or female cousin—must carry out a rite in their memory, of constantly carrying a small wooden statuette representing the dead child, and looking after the statuette as if it were alive. Failure to do this is punished by a curse. The girl's grandmother, at the back of the shrine, is a Vodun priestess in the service of Mami Wata. When the photograph was taken, the women proudly exposed their breasts, explaining that the goddess preferred servants with large breasts as symbols of fertility and abundance. (According to legend the goddess herself had very large breasts, but was a proud and touchy woman who would not allow any comments on her physique. One day, her husband drank a little too much palm wine and made an unkind remark on the subject. She stamped on the floor in anger and turned into a river to return home to her father.)

Anfouin, Togo

TWINS SHARE A SOUL

This woman's twins became deities when they died. She must always carry these two *ibeji* statues, which represent the deceased children, wherever she goes: to the market, the beach, or on journeys. She does not consider her twins to be dead, but cares for them, washing them with water infused with herbs to protect their health. Every evening, she kisses them and prays for them.

Twins are viewed differently throughout Africa. They are worshipped throughout the Gulf of Benin, where they are believed to have two fathers, one physical and one spiritual. The Yoruba believe that twins share one soul, and if one twin dies, the other loses his soul and also dies. In northern Togo, however; twins are a sign of bad luck.

Lome, Togo

EXORCISM OF A CHILD

This child is believed to be suffering from an evil spell that is stopping him from sleeping. Because of a land dispute, a neighbor is believed to have wreaked revenge by casting a spell over the child—more vulnerable than an adult—and through him, the whole family. The child's parents have brought him to the Vodun priest to remove the spell.

The first step to curing the child is to find out what the family has done wrong—in Africa, there is always a link between sickness and wrong behavior. If the child is not cured immediately, his whole family will fall ill because of their guilt. To remove the curse, the priest consults the oracle to ask whether an exorcism might be dangerous, as spells have been known to turn against the priest carrying out the exorcism. In preparation, a chalk circle is drawn around the child to trap the evil leaving the child's spirit. To placate the earth, some alcohol is poured on the ground, and to appease the vodun, the priest sacrifices some chickens and a young goat. The ceremony can then begin. It lasts all night, finishing with an immersion in the ocean, and the child is cured. As if by magic, the evil that possessed the child's spirit is transferred into a bottle placed inside the chalk circle.

Amoutivie neighborhood, Lome, Togo

A VODUN ALTAR

This priestess is praying in front of an altar devoted to Mami Wata. It stands in the back of the shrine, in a space next to the main room, where the Vodun ceremonies are held. The altar is made of various pieces of bric-a-brac gathered by the priestess, such as statuettes of the Hindu god Shiva, animal horns, bottles of cloudy liquid, shells, and wooden carvings. These disparate objects have one thing in common: they are devoted to the worship of Mami Wata, whose faith incorporates Hindu gods as readily as African fetishes. Mami Wata is worshipped mainly along the coast in Ghana, Togo, and Benin, where the first white settlers lived in the sixteenth century. The influence of these white settlers is apparent in the worship of Mami Wata, for whom anything related to Europeans is very powerful.

Togo

THE FETISH OF THE SACRED FOREST

These young vodun-si are taking part in celebrations in the sacred forest of Be, the most important Vodun site in Togo. The celebrations last four days and are held in honor of the leopard, the forest's powerful guardian. Only the high priest is allowed to enter the forest fully clothed; all other worshippers must be bare-breasted as a sign of humility, with only necklaces and cloth wraps permitted. The worshippers follow the rhythm of the singing by clapping as they dance—the forest's fetish, one of the most powerful in the whole region, hates the sound of drums and anything else that recalls the modern world. Because of this no electricity or running water, or any other modern inventions, are allowed in the forest.

Sacred Forest of Be, Lome, Togo

SAKPATA, GOD OF DISEASE

These children are ill and have come to this Vodun convent in Benin to seek a cure. The white marks on their bodies represent Sakpata, god of smallpox and other contagious diseases. They are about to sacrifice chickens to Sakpata to free them of disease and bring them to salvation. Once they are cured, they will be in Sakpata's service for the rest of their lives.

During colonization, the British banned the Vodun religion in Nigeria, fearing that its followers deliberately spread smallpox, but worship of Sakpata continued in secret. The kings of Dahomey—modern-day Benin—were so terrified of smallpox that they forbade Sakpata's priests to go into town, in case they caught it and introduced it to the palace. These priests continue to be much in demand and, since the eradication of smallpox, they have specialized in other diseases.

Benin

A YOUNG MAN CARRYING
A VODUN ON HIS SHOULDERS

Achinas kpon are heavy burdens decorated with feathers and filled with sacred objects that channel the power of the vodun. During ceremonies, initiates pray, sing, and dance to invoke the voduns, messengers of Mawu, the sexless supreme being who rules the universe. The deities come down to earth and possess the bodies and spirits of the worshippers, who go into a trance. These channelers become gods and can talk with other worshippers present at the ceremony. People tell about their problems and ask the voduns to intercede with Mawu on their behalf. When a worshipper is possessed in this way, he carries the *achinas kpon* to show the others that he is no longer human, but a god.

Ouidah, Benin

VODUN FLAGS

Messengers carrying flags in the colors of their voduns parade through the streets to announce the new members of their congregation. The worshippers dance in the town square to the sound of drums. If a child goes into a trance during this ceremony, it is a clear sign that he or she has been chosen to serve a deity. The child is shut in a room in the convent until the end of the initiation period. No one—neither the parents, nor the child's school—can oppose the deity's choice.

Gliji, Togo

EYES ROLLED UPWARDS

This man is in a trance, battling witches who are trying to interrupt the funeral of an Ashanti chief so that he cannot rest in peace. To fight the witches, the man must try to enter their world, which is the opposite of ours. His eyes are rolled upwards in an effort to unmask the witches. Witches do everything the opposite from humans: they walk backwards on their heads, begin sentences at the end, rest during the day, go out at night, and hang from tree branches to sleep. Above all, they are the opposite of humans because their goal is harm and destruction.

Ghana

SPIRITS HAVE NO FACE

This worshipper is resting in a courtyard between two dances during a great Vodun ceremony. On his head is a bundle of red cloth decorated with parrot feathers. He hides his face when he dances so that the spirit of the ancestors will protect his identity and his inner nature. Spirits have no faces.

The three men standing behind him are his constant companions. They are there to protect him. If a violent deity begins to "ride" him during the ritual, they intervene to make sure the deity does not harm him or anyone else.

Ouidah, Benin

THE FA ORACLE

Fa is the art of divination. In Fa philosophy, the world was created from various combinations of the four elements: earth, air, fire, and water. Each sign, linked to one of these elements, forms a spiritual bond with a deity who explains life and gives advice to believers, who consult the Fa oracle at every major step of their life and to ask questions of the voduns. This priest and soothsayer stands in front of his room full of oracles.

The oracle reads the message using cola nuts. According to legend the first soothsayer went into the sacred forest of Ife in Nigeria. He sat under a palm tree with sixteen branches surrounded by sixteen holes into each of which fell sixteen nuts. The 256 nuts represent the number of signs the Fa oracle has to interpret. Each sign is a code consisting of sixteen proverbs and sixteen legends, giving a total of 65,536 possible combinations.

Ouidah, Benin

FOREIGN IS GOOD

For this Ewe worshipper from southern Togo, a plastic doll is an important ritual tool. It symbolizes modern life, which interests certain voduns, and, just like wooden or stone statuettes, it also represents man. The fact that the doll is white and imported from abroad makes it especially powerful and prestigious. In this part of the Gulf of Benin, Africans have always traded with Europeans, and for this reason wealth is often seen as coming from overseas. As a result, imported goods are considered particularly beneficial.

Togo

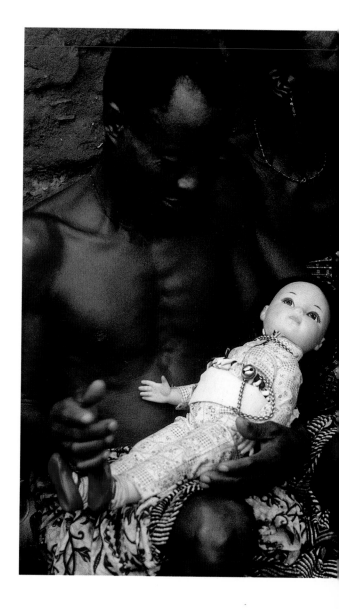

THE PROPHET SPEAKING TO GOD

This man is communicating directly with God, who comes to him when he is alone, in a halo of light resembling the headlights on a truck. God orders him to combat Satan, witches, and other fetish priests who tempt men with *gri-gris* (charms) and magic amulets. The prophet travels from village to village to save souls, which are torn between good and evil, light and darkness, and are under constant attack from the devil and his army of demons. When the prophet arrives in a village people; volunteer to undergo baptism. He throws their ritual tools and fetishes at his feet to save them. He then prays and sprinkles the newly converted Christians with holy water, before reading the Bible to an ecstatic crowd. The prophet will explain that incurable diseases, failed harvests, poverty, and all natural ills are caused by evil spirits, and that the cross is the final rampart protecting the world, whose power terrifies witches and demons, and destroys the devil.

This man is just one of many prophets active throughout Africa. Some found their own church, such as the Celestial Christian Church in Benin, the Harrist Church in Ivory Coast, and the Kibanguist Church in the Democratic Republic of Congo. Living on the margins of the society, many end up in prison, or are simply forgotten.

Ivory Coast

THE PROPHET SAMUEL

Samuel is a preacher from Ivory Coast. Eight years ago, he had a mystic revelation, in which the sky tore open with a halo of light and an African riding a black horse appeared and called Samuel by his name. The horseman was God, and He ordered Samuel to travel across Africa on foot, preaching Christianity wherever he went. Samuel left his native village, abandoning his family, and has been walking and preaching ever since. All he owns is his long robe, a wooden cross, and an old Bible. He lives by begging and sleeps out in the open. He is one of many such prophets, and believes he has been sent to save Africa from evil in the form of witchcraft, animism, and traditional African faith.

Conakry, Guinea

SPIRITS AND DEITIES

These two young women are in a trance, communicating directly with higher spirits. The dividing line between deities and spirits is very thin. The former—voduns or orishas—live far from this world and close to the supreme being of creation. They make their presence felt in sun, rain, storms, and wind. They appear to men only rarely to call on their service. Spirits, on the other hand, are close to men and share their daily life. Although they are invisible, they are omnipresent in nature, in forests, rivers, and mountains. In case of catastrophes such as epidemics or natural disasters, men try to contact the gods. But, for everyday problems such as neighborhood disputes, minor accidents, or illness, they prefer to call on the spirits of ancestors or nature.

Mono, Benin

THE PALANQUIN AND THE POWER OF THE VODUN

In Benin, only the king may travel in a palanquin. It is a sign of wealth and power, demonstrating that the sovereign is closer to the gods than his subjects. This mark of respect is also shown to vodun-si at the end of their initiation period. (The fly whisks they are holding are another symbol of royal power.) The palanquin raises the initiates above the heads of the crowd, symbolically placing them between heaven and earth. On leaving the convent, as soon as the cortege begins to move, the two initiates fall into a trance of possession, indicating that they are no longer women but voduns.

Benin

VODUN-TRON GODS ARE SHY

These women are wearing the attire of the gods who have possessed them in order to communicate with their believers. The mask characterizes a very violent god, inspired by wrestling matches the priest has seen on television. This new religion, Vodun-tron, is very fashionable in larger towns and cities in Benin and Togo, and involves Vodun rituals that have been adapted to modern life. For example, women are allowed to wear bras during the rituals, where formerly they would have been bare-breasted. Similarly, the services are held not as the traditional Vodun calendar dictates but according to office or factory hours. In Lome, for example, services are held on Saturday evenings and Sunday afternoons, while major celebrations take place during the school holidays. However, the biggest change beween the old and new forms of ritual has been in the relationship between individual worshippers and the gods. The spiritual approach of Vodun has been radically altered, becoming an all-inclusive ritual. The leader takes his inspiration from other religions, daily life, television, and cinema, to create an original service in line with the demands of modern life. The gods, through the Tron priests, typically demand ample payment for their intercession, which might involve finding a job for an unemployed man, increasing trade for a business, or helping a student succeed in his exams.

Be neighborhood, Lome, Togo

THE CHRISTIAN CROSS PLAYS
A PART IN VODUN CEREMONIES

In large African cities, Islam and Christianity are more preva-
lent than traditional African beliefs. Vodun has adapted
accordingly, in order to survive. The Vodun-tron religion
incorporates elements of the Christian liturgy. Services are
held on a Sunday, and the Christian cross is a commonly
found symbol, even on Vodun worshippers' clothes.

Lome, Togo

VODUN AS IMPROVISED THEATER

This initiate of the Vodun-tron faith is possessed by Legba,
protector of villages and roads. Unlike the goddess Fa, who
fixes individual destinies, Legba has the power to change
the course of men's lives. Legba is a major god, who enjoys
playing tricks and causing chaos, both among men and
gods. He is sly, wily, and impulsive. He can both reward and
punish men; it all depends on his mood, which is mercurial
and unpredictable. He flits between the two worlds, with one
foot on the earth, and the other in heaven, and because of
this, his legs are unequal length.

   This young woman has taken on Legba's limp as well as
his gravelly male voice. She jokes with the crowd, plays
tricks, and becomes angry without reason. The service is a
performance in which the gods act their own roles. The
ceremony lasts over eight hours, with the voduns "riding"
the bodies of the possessed to act out their characters.

Lome, Togo

THE PHALLUS DANCE

This vodun-si is entertaining the congregation by miming sexual intercourse with an ebony phallus. She is symbolically fertilizing the seed sown by the peasants to ensure a good harvest. The phallus also symbolizes virility. When an infertile woman wants to become pregnant, she uses phallic statuettes in a vodun ritual in honor of the god Legba, who is often represented with a gigantic phallus. Most infertile women consult a *bokonon* (soothsayer), or priest who has studied magic. The *bokonon* will consult the spirits in the bush and makes her a *bo*, or amulet, which will help her become pregnant.

Glidji, Togo

KOKU WORSHIPPERS

This woman is possessed by Koku, god of battles, who fights witches and black magic. He is very popular throughout the Gulf of Benin, and spectacular ceremonies are held in his honor. His worshippers wear raffia skirts and smear their bodies with *jassi*, a thick paste made of manioc flour, palm oil, and various plants reputed to bestow invincibility. Worshippers possessed by Koku whip themselves into a frenzy. The god is a bloodthirsty figure who encourages his followers to cut themselves with knives or broken bottles to prepare themselves to fight witches.

Benin

POSSESSION BY A DEITY

These women have just been possessed by a deity. Their
temperatures rose sharply during the possession and are
now returning to normal. They are somewhat dazed and
cannot remember what they did during the trance, and the
women are gradually returning to themselves, as though
coming round after being intoxicated. The period of forget-
fulness that follows a possession is a key part of the mystic
aura of the possessed state. No one can remember being a
deity, even a few minutes after the possession ends.

Near Allada, Benin

A THIRST FOR BLOOD

This man is looking for a young goat so he can drink its
blood, the sacred drink of Ogun, the orisha possessing him.
Ogun is the god of iron and of war. Legend has it that it was
Ogun's machete that cut the paths that first made the earth
habitable for men. Ogun is one of the principal orishas of the
Vodun pantheon. He is the patron vodun of smiths, soldiers,
truck and taxi drivers, railway workers, and anyone who
works with metal. He is considered the most just of all the
gods and thus presides over trade agreements, notaries,
and contracts. In court, his believers do not swear on the
Bible, but on iron. Ogun demands blood in his ceremonies.

THE GODS ENJOY MUSIC

Musical instruments and rhythmic drumming play a vital role in Vodun rituals. Quite simply, there can be no ceremony without music—the gods react when music is played and do not like silent prayer. During services, priests call down the gods with sacred songs, dancing, and drumming. As the tempo increases, the voduns appear, and each sudden change in tempo causes people to fall into a trance. Before speaking to the congregation, the gods dance with men to the constant accompaniment of music. Several deities may "ride" the worshippers.

Togo

VODUNS LOVE SCHNAPPS

This ceremony has been at the same pitch of intensity since it began over sixteen hours ago. A convent has brought its vodun—its fetish in a jar covered with palm leaves—into town. A woman in a trance carries the jar on her head. At each stop, the priest sprinkles her face with schnapps, and people in the crowd fall into a trance. In Togo, voduns love alcohol, with a particular fondness for Dutch schnapps.

Anfouin, Togo

THE ROLE OF PLASTIC TOYS IN RITUAL

Each September, this coastal town hosts the ceremonies of the Sacred Stone, marking the beginning of the Vodun calendar. High priests come from all over southern Togo to take part in a complex ritual to reveal the color of a rock hidden in the shrine. If the rock is white, all is well. If it is black, calamity will strike the country. The priests bring Japanese dolls and toys to the ceremony as a way of showing off their social status. These *bocios* are used only in certain ceremonies, in rituals to attract money, prosperity, and power. Such imported goods, particularly from wealthy countries, are very popular and may include plastic dolls, soft toys, electronic toys, baby powder, and perfume.

Aneho, Togo

112

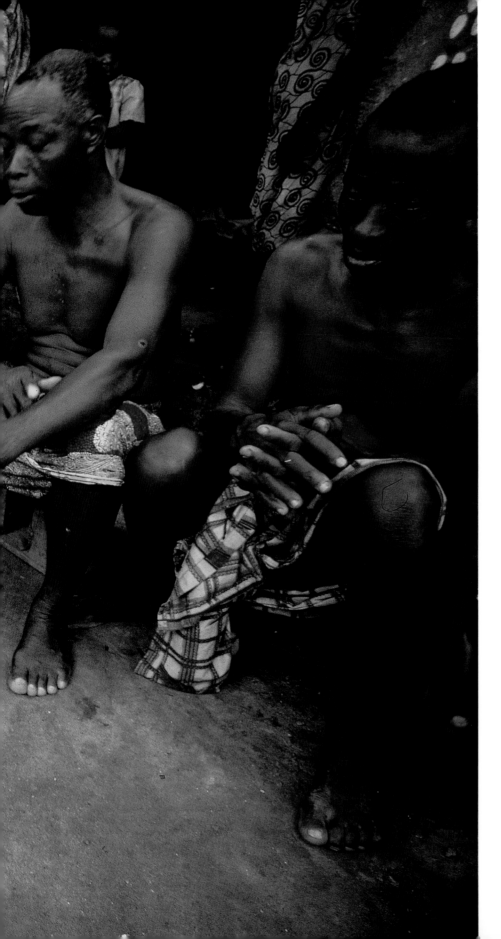

SECRECY IS AT THE HEART OF THE VODUN FAITH

These novices have just completed three months of initiation in a vodun convent. They have sworn to keep the secrets taught by the *midawo* (high priest), who warns them that if they tell what they have seen and learned, the vodun will kill them.

Vodun rituals are shrouded in mystery. At every stage of their initiation, novices are taught that their lives are under constant threat from evil spirits. Only their faith in Vodun deities and knowledge of their secrets can protect them from harm. During their mystical seclusion, these young girls have learned how to keep secrets. They have also studied how to draw down lightning, cure infectious diseases, resolve conflicts, mete out divine justice, and punish criminals. When they become vodun-si, they swear not to kill, lie, or practice witchcraft, and to honor the convent's deities every day. With their new status they must be respected, and if someone does them wrong, they are obliged to scream and cry until the wrongdoer apologizes, even if it takes several days. Those who do not apologize will be punished by the vodun.

Aneho region, Togo

SOOTHSAYERS ARE CHOSEN
BEFORE BIRTH

This three-year-old girl from Togo is destined to study the art of Fa divination, found in countries along the Gulf of Benin. Children are often destined to become oracles even before birth. The mother-to-be will go to the *bokonon* (soothsayer) to ask about the personality and identity of her baby and, a few days later, she will receive the child's *fa*, or fate. When the oracle chooses a child to be a soothsayer, the mother-to-be makes sacrifices and takes part in cere-monies, seeing herself as part of the child's soul and destiny. She follows rules forbidding certain foods, cleans herself with plants, and wears jewelry for protection. She must also wear the colors that the child will wear throughout its life. When the child reaches the age of seven, he or she goes to the soothsayer to study Fa divination. It takes a year to learn the principal signs, and another three years to learn the secondary signs. When the child is twelve, he or she will learn to interpret the different systems and, after a few more years of study, will leave the master to practice their skills with other soothsayers. When they are thirty or forty, they may become a *bokonon* in their own right.

Togo

SAINT MICHAEL IN THE ROLE OF OGUN, GOD OF WAR AND IRON

This child is standing in front of an image of Saint Michael the Archangel, carved on one of the church doors of the Society of Cherubim and Seraphim. Like members of the Celestial Church in Benin, these fundamentalist Christians combat orisha and vodun worship. Their struggle is somewhat paradoxical because their religious practices are inspired as much by these two faiths as by the Bible. The followers of the Society of Cherubim and Seraphim believe in holy visions similar to those believed by the Yoruba and Ewe. For them, the Christian saints perform the same role as orishas and voduns, and, arguably, only the names have changed. Saint Michael is Ogun, god of iron and war; Saint Anthony is Legba, protector of roads. The offerings of fruit, the burning candles, incense, holy anointing oil, and purification of holy water in this church are all inspired by the African faiths that they aim to destroy.

Lagos, Nigeria

CELESTIAL CHRISTIANS FIGHTING VODUN INFLUENCE

This young girl, a member of the Celestial Christian Church, is praying to fight the voduns in her neighborhood. In 1947, a carpenter by the name of Samuel Oshoffa set himself up as a prophet after receiving instructions from God to found his own church. This holy vision led to the creation of a community of twelve million Christians across Benin, Nigeria, Togo, and Ghana. The avowed aim of the church is to combat evil— seen in this region to be incarnated by Vodun. The church's liturgy begins by stating that the Celestial Christian Church is the last lifeboat and that anyone who does not climb aboard will drown in deep waters. The church's dignitaries, called "visionaries," receive messages directly from God, and when a member of the congregation goes into a trance during mass, he or she begins speaking in tongues. The incomprehensible speech produced is called "the language of the angels" and is carefully transcribed and interpreted as a divine revelation. Celestial Christians follow twelve commandments, which state that colored candles, alcohol, pork, and tobacco are expressly forbidden in church. It is also forbidden to worship vodun, practice black magic, commit adultery, and wear red or black clothing. In church, women, who must never enter the church while menstruating, worship separately from men.

Saint-Maur, France

SPIRITS HIDING IN THE BUSH

The bush is filled with evil spirits who can consider-able harm. People rarely venture out into the bush alone. Every year, the Ewe of southern Ghana organize rituals in honor of the spirits of the bush, represented by costumes covered with leaves.

Near Anlo, Ghana

PUNISHMENT OF CRIMINALS

In Togo, justice is often meted out by Vodun priests. Here, a radio has just been stolen from this Lome store, where several families live. To find the thief, the fetish priest has brought together the twenty-eight people who live here. He digs a hole in the ground and ties a rope bound to a walnut around each person's neck and wrists. He throws the nut into the hole and buries it. Each person kneels in turn in front of the *bocios* and submits to the priest's interrogation. Anyone telling the truth can stand back up with no difficulty. However, this young girl is lying. She is guilty, and the rope is pulling her down to the ground. If she does not admit her theft, she will be strangled.

Africa is home to several such types of divine ordeal. In Ivory Coast, for instance, a substance is poured into the eyes of the accused. Only those who are guilty are blinded. Elsewhere, the guilty party dies after being given poison, or suspects are tied by the hands and feet and thrown into water. Drowning is proof of their guilt. Fire is also a tradi-tional instrument of justice: an innocent man can walk through fire or grasp a white-hot object without being burned.

Be neighborhood, Lome, Togo

NIGERIAN BUSINESSMEN

These two British men, resident in Nigeria, have been named traditional chiefs under the king of Oyo. This title gives them duties to the sovereign but also grants them certain rights, among them the right to trade. The Yoruba of southwestern Nigeria refuse to allow foreigners to create businesses without permission from the traditional authorities—in other words, the gods. Anyone who does not request permission before starting their business is doomed to fail. An American who recently opened a hotel here learned this to his own cost: his rooms remained empty until he paid for a ceremony honoring the regional gods.

Nigeria

WESTERNERS INITIATED INTO VODUN

Priests of some of the recent Vodun-tron religions in fashion in Benin adapt their rituals to attract a new type of worshipper—wealthy Europeans looking for excitement. The complexity of the initiation ceremony depends on the price Western "customers" are willing to pay. The priest has painted his face with imaginary symbols to play the part. His necklace, hat, and loincloth have no religious significance but are merely part of a costume designed to impress the French client standing behind him. The priest has given himself an extremely grand-sounding title: "Founding President, Minister of Afro-American Culture, Coordinator of African Totemic Geography, Permanent Secretary of the High Council of the Hwendo Voodoo Faith, and Member of the Alafia-Gbedida-UNESCO NGO Commission." Today, in large towns and cities across Africa, Vodun has become a source of profit. Fetishes are on sale, and those who buy them can found their own religion, charging for every ceremony they host.

Cotonou, Benin

THE GODDESS OF WATER

This priest, assisted by vodun-si, is a leading dignitary of the Vodun faith. He is in a shrine dedicated to Mami Wata, the goddess of water, who loves spotless clothes, perfumes, jewelry, and general cleanliness. Shrines to Mami Wata, whose name comes from the pidgin term "Mammy Water," are cleaned several times a day. The goddess hates alcohol and tobacco, but when she possesses a worshipper, she sometimes laughs and stumbles in their body as if drunk.

Mami Wata is very popular among female traders, particularly the wealthy *nana-benz*, who sell the traditional cloth wraps known as *pagnes* in the central marketplace in Lome. Mami Wata attracts worshippers who feel torn between African traditions and material comforts imported from abroad. She encourages social success, individualism, power, and wealth. The Ewe created the figure of Mami Wata when the first wealthy powerful Europeans landed in West Africa. She is a mix of water spirits from earlier forms of water worship and European, Indian, and African influences. She was given the form of the mermaids that decorated ships' prows as figureheads, and was associated with wealth from the sea. Today, she is worshipped by people seeking prosperity, as well as by those seeking an identity in the melting pot of modern African culture.

Aneho, Togo

BEAUTIFUL MAMI WATA

This woman is about to be appointed mama-si, priestess in the service of Mami Wata, goddess of water. She has put on her finest ritual garb to please the deity, who loves everything that is beautiful and peaceful. Mami Wata's favorite color is white and her worshippers cover themselves with talc and perfume during ceremonies in her honor. Mami Wata appears in dreams as an extremely beautiful woman with a pale complexion and long hair. She is often accompanied by multi-colored snakes. Sometimes she is nude, covered in jewels, or possesses a fish's tail like a mermaid. Her worshippers decorate her altar with bottles of perfume, soft drinks, Catholic statuettes, crucifixes, and Indian or Buddhist deities. Mirrors are also used as decoration, because these represent the surface of the water, separating the ocean where the goddess lives from the land, where men live.

Lome, Togo

SPIRITUAL TRANSFORMATION

This servant to a *sangoma* (Xhosa soothsayer) is kneeling in front of her mistress, as a sign of submission and respect. She has painted her body to indicate that she is undergoing a spiritual transformation to become a sangoma herself.

Sangomas are intermediaries between the world of spirits and the world of the living. They are at once seers, healers, ritual priests, psychologists, and sometimes even detectives (they have been known to find lost herds of cattle). Under the apartheid regime, they made *muti* (magic remedy) talismans for ANC fighters. During certain ceremonies, they go into a trance and have political visions. Sangomas are also responsible for unmasking witches. Occasionally, as with *griots* from Guinea, they narrate the history and customs of the black peoples of South Africa. There are estimated to be some 230,000 *sangomas* in South Africa, and 84 percent of the population is estimated to consult one at least three times a year.

Bizana, Transkei, South Africa

THE SANGOMA THROWS HER VOICE

The sangoma's sophisticated attire is designed to impress onlookers and to show that she is on excellent terms with the ancestors. She holds divination sessions in public, dancing herself into a trance and contacting the spirits. To impress her audience, she alters her voice and begins a ritual dialogue with another mysterious voice, relying on her powers of ventriloquism. People come to consult the sangoma mainly on issues related to the practice of witch-craft, widely believed to cause problems such as unexplained ailments, persistent ill fortune, painful menstrual cramps, and miscarriages. The sangoma treats these with traditional medicine based on colors, to restore harmony between the patient and his or her surroundings. She symbolically mixes opposites to unite them: light colors represent life and masculinity; dark colors are death and femininity. White medicine represents health, purity, success, and healing, while black medicine represents night, danger, and hardship. Red symbolizes the bridge between black and white. The patient is therefore given black medicine to remove the ailment; red to begin the process of healing; then white to complete the cure and give strength and energy.

Libode, Transkei, South Africa

FETISHES FROM THE FAR SIDE OF THE UNIVERSE

Kokue is one of the greatest Vodun fetish priests in Lome, the capital of Togo. People come to seek his help to find stolen goods, resolve conflicts, prove their husband or wife is being unfaithful, cure ailments, pass an exam, and so on. For each consultation, he wears his ritual attire covered in *gri-gris*. These charms protect him from the evil spirits who assail him every time he intercedes with the gods on someone's behalf. They make him invulnerable and assure him of victory over the witches who constantly try to steal his powers. This *gri-gris* armor, handed down from father to son, is believed to be extremely effective because the amulets were all made by Muslims, considered to live on the far side of the universe. The charms are made from a variety of materials: wood, hair, bone and, especially, verses from the Koran.

Lome, Togo

NDEBELE NECKLACES

Married Ndebele women wear thick rings of beads, called *iirholwana*, round their ankles, calves, wrists, neck, and waist. *lindzila* are the traditional rings that all Ndebele women wear round their neck and legs. They were originally made of copper, and could not be removed, but today they are usually gold-colored plastic, and can be taken off at any time. The woman in the foreground is wearing a traditional copper necklace that she cannot remove. The women believe that their jewelry protects them against evil spirits.

South Africa

BECOMING A WOMAN

To hold their community together and to keep a close bond with their culture, most young Ndebele women undergo an initiation rite that will make them "real women." Shortly before the full moon, the young women are taken to a secret place where their head and body hair are shaved to represent their return to nature. They are given a ritual bath and covered with a blanket. Women who have already undergone initiation then strip naked and begin a rite, which involves joking about men and their genitalia and simulating ritual sex acts with the girls. In the morning, the girls return to their community for a month, during which time they are kept at home and are not allowed to come into contact with men. At the end of the month, their blankets and initiatory garments are burned to symbolize their passage into adulthood, and they are allowed to wear a bead apron representing womanhood.

Near Middelburg, South Africa

THE CURSE OF THE GCALEKA
OF SOUTH AFRICA

These two sangomas live among the Gcaleka clan. Every year on February 18, they hold an exorcism to cleanse the clan spiritually of a curse that struck them over a century ago, when a fourteen-year-old girl called Nongqawuse received a message from her ancestors as she sat by a pond, their faces reflected in the water. These ancestors predicted that a powerful wind would sweep the white colonists into the sea if the Xhosa made a sacrifice. The ancestors demanded each family's herds or crops, and threatened that those who refused would be turned into a mouse, a frog, or an ant. For ten months, the Gcaleka and Xhosa were seized by a sort of group hysteria, killing their cattle and burning their crops. On February 18, 1857, the day when the prophecy was supposed to come true, the wind failed to materialize; as a result of the destruction, twenty-five thousand Xhosa starved to death. The girl, known as the South African Joan of Arc, had to flee and seek protection with the white colonists. She sought refuge on Robben Island, where Nelson Mandela was later held prisoner.

Transkei, South Africa

RITUAL MURDERS AND MAGIC CHARMS

Helene Makwiya lives in Soweto. She paints white spots on her body to protect herself from evil spirits. Three years ago, she was forced to flee her village in the Transvaal region after her house was set on fire by a crazed mob who accused her of witchcraft. Her husband's mistress had started the rumor that Helene was a witch making *mutis* to kill her. In a ten-year period, more than six hundred so-called witches have been killed in this province—many more if ritual murders are included in the count.

Ritual murders are carried out to harvest the body parts needed to make *mutis*. A hand buried at the entrance to a store, for example, is thought to bring in customers; male genitalia are thought to increase virility and fertility; and stomach fat guarantees a good harvest. According to tradition, *mutis* are considered to be more effective if the body parts are taken from living children, because their screams awaken the supernatural powers.

Soweto, South Africa

SOUTH AFRICAN ZIONIST CHRISTIANS

This young girl has just joined the Zionist Christian Church. Members of the congregation are walking around her singing in a classroom that has been temporarily transformed into a church. She will now have to promise to follow all the church's precepts: no smoking, no drinking, no lying, and sexual abstinence prior to church ceremonies. Members of this independent South African church are very popular among employers, thanks to their honesty, loyalty, and punctuality.

Soweto, South Africa

"WHEN AN ELDER DIES…"

In the Transkei region of South Africa, the oldest member of the family is its spiritual guide, responsible for telling the Xhosa creation myth. Africans have a saying that the teachings of a wise elder are more precious than religious initiation. As the well-known thinker Amadou Hampâté Bâ, a native of Mali, wrote, "When an elder dies, a library is lost forever."

Transkei, South Africa

STONING FOR THOSE ACCUSED OF WITCHCRAFT

These are sangomas, outside their traditional houses. In the past, an initiation period of ten to twenty-five years was needed to become a sangoma in South Africa. Today, the period of initiation only lasts a few years or even just a few months. The tradition is crumbling, and its customs all but vanished.

The activities of Christian and Muslim missionaries are having a major impact on the reputations of these traditional soothsayers. They are caricatured in the media and are frequently accused of crimes related to witchcraft. In South Africa, in a period of less than a year, nearly one hundred and fifty women and men were accused of being diabolic sangomas or witches. All were summarily stoned to death, without trial, by villagers.

Near Umtata, Transkei, South Africa

DREAMS AS CURE

For these young Pondos, from Transkei in South Africa, to become sangomas, they must cure the secret ailment inherited from their ancestors. This test is principally faced by women. During a long period of initiation, they must uncover the ill gnawing away at them and confess the faults that have caused the wrath of their ancestors. The young initiates will be cured when they dream of a wild animal such as a lion, panther, or elephant. This animal, called an *ytyala*, is an incarnation of the ancestor responsible for the ailment. The ancestor will then authorize the cure, ending the period of initiation. Throughout the initiation, the young women live together in a hut. If they go into town, their bodies must be painted with white chalk to indicate that they are journeying between the realm of the ancestors and the world of the living.

Near Port Saint John's, Transkei, South Africa

WHITE SYMBOLIZES MORAL RECTITUDE

Xhosa men smear their face and body with white clay during initiation to protect themselves from the devil. The light emitted by the pale color is believed to drive away evil spirits. At the end of the initiation period, the young man must wash in the river to symbolize his entrance into manhood.

Transkei, South Africa

WHITE, THE COLOR OF REBIRTH

In South Africa, as in most of Africa, white is the color of transformation and is the sacred color of God. (In some regions, however, white symbolizes death.) These initiates have painted their skin white to symbolize their spiritual rebirth. Today the paint is made from kaolin clay or crushed chalk, but in the past it was made from ground egg or snail shells or lizard excrement.

Transkei, South Africa

THE ZIONIST CHRISTIAN CHURCH

The Zionist Christian Church (ZCC) in South Africa is nearly a century old, and was founded by a black farm laborer who named his new church after Mount Zion near Jerusalem. It seeks its members from the poor black communities living in the townships, and is the largest of the independent—i.e. non-white—African churches. Members wear a star pinned to their chest or the cap they wear with their uniform.

During the apartheid era, a part of the white Afrikaner Church rejected the black population, claiming that blacks had no soul and should not be allowed to join the Christian fellowship. Today, the ZCC is led by a bishop who is considered an intermediary between God and men. His followers see him as a prophet with supernatural powers.

Moria, South Africa

JUMPING AS AN AID TO PRAYER

The *mokhukhus* are the main group of men within the South African Zionist Christian Church. Like all followers of the faith, they follow its precepts scrupulously, particularly the unique way of praying: to come closer to God and to pour all their energy into their faith, *mokhukhus* jump and clap. Each time they jump, they focus on trying to fly symbolically up to God, and each time they come back down to the ground, they slap the floor noisily with their oversized white shoes, called *manyanyathas*. Prayer is conducted several times a week, with an eight-hour stretch on Saturdays, from eleven in the morning to seven in the evening. To keep going, the faithful drink tea-flavored holy water called *mogabolo*.

Moria, South Africa

FEAR OF WITCHES

In the Transkei province in South Africa, Mpondomise witches are held responsible for all unexplained ills, including accidents, tornadoes, storms, and epidemics such as leprosy or AIDS. They are likewise blamed for disfiguring diseases, such as scabies or elephantiasis, and for blindness, deafness, impotence, and infertility. They are accused of inciting theft, alcohol abuse, adultery—in short, anything that upsets the harmony and order of the world.

Witches have powers that they can transfer to objects or foodstuffs, and therefore it is possible to become a witch without being aware of it, simply by eating contaminated food or picking up an "impure" object. When villagers discover a witch in their midst, she—it is nearly always a woman—is condemned to death by stoning or being buried alive.

Near Qumbu, Transkei, South Africa

THE *GRIOTTE'S* STORY

Like their male counterparts, these *griottes* would once have been in the service of a monarch or great family, and sung the exploits of their protectors. Today, many of these women have become great stars in their home countries. Although they no longer sing the glories of great Mandingo rulers, they do recite poetry in praise of noble families and command high prices at weddings to recount the history of the couple about to marry.

Senegal

THE *BALAFON* XYLOPHONE

The *balafon* is not just a musical instrument, but is an important symbol: for example, in Burkina Faso, only *griots* who have led a successful life are permitted to play the large *balafon* at funerals. For a man, a successful life means being married and having plenty of children, being a good hunter, and having a full grain store and plenty of cattle. Unmarried adults and children are only allowed to play a small *balafon*.

Other traditional instruments played by *griots* are the *kora* (a harp made from a calabash with over twenty strings) and the *ntamanin* (a small drum held beneath the upper arm). These days, *griots* often sing and perform amplified music, inspiring much modern African music.

Burkina Faso

THE *GRIOT'S* SONG

Through the generations, it was common for a *griot* (a member of the musician caste) family (to be attached to a noble family who protected and fed its members. In exchange, the *griot* was expected to pass along knowledge of the genealogy and dynastic traditions of his protectors, helping to spread their fame and to garner their praises. The role was also similar to that of a medieval court jester. The king called on his *griots* as advisers, messengers, and spokesmen, because important chiefs never spoke directly to their subjects or inferiors.

Although *griots* were not allowed to bear arms, they accompanied the king on the battlefield, to urge him on by recounting the great feats of his ancestors. The epics told by the *griots* typically used very high-flown language and imagery and could be several thousand lines long. The most famous of these epics, the Mandingo epic of King Sundiata Keita, recounting the creation of the Mali Empire, exists in over twenty different versions.

Gambia

GRIOTS AND THE MUSICAL TRADITION

Griots belong to the musician caste in West Africa. They are found throughout Mali, Senegal, Gambia, and to a lesser extent in other countries in the region. In these countries, society is traditionally divided into three hierarchical ranks. The highest, which represents most of the population, are the noble or the free, and are generally crop or livestock farmers. Then comes the caste class, which includes various sorts of craftsmen, such as smiths, carpenters, shoemakers, weavers, and potters, as well as *griots*. The third class, which is now disappearing, consists of slaves and their descendants. In Nigeria's many royal courts, there are still many families of slaves belonging to the sovereign.

Nigeria

THE BWITI CEREMONY
AND THE ROLE OF WOMEN

At the start of each Bwiti ceremony, a member of the congregation purifies the shrine with a lit torch. This ritual is found among the Fang and Mitsogho people of Gabon, Cameroon, and Equatorial Guinea. Among the Mitsogho, only men are initiated into the faith as they alone are guardians of the mystic revelation at the heart of the Bwiti religion. During initiation, any man who fails to "journey through the realm of death" to see the Bwiti is considered a woman and is turned away from the ritual. Before a man is initiated, he stands to the left of the shrine, the side considered dark and dangerous and usually reserved for women. It is symbolized by the moon. Once the man has seen the Bwiti and passed the initiation test, he goes and stands among the men on the right, on the side symbolizing light, life, and the sun.

Near Libreville, Gabon

"ANGELS" UNDER THE INFLUENCE

These *banzies* (angels) are followers of the Bwiti faith. They have not slept for fifty-two hours. To keep going during this long ritual, singing and dancing without sleep for the entire weekend, they drink a potion made from iboga, a powerful hallucinogen. This ceremony involves acting out the creation myth and lasts three nights. To symbolize birth, the *banzies* wear red, the color of the blood of childbirth. Death is symbolized by blue clothing and rebirth by white. The ceremony sometimes also plays out the life of Christ, or the history of the Fang people: colonization, the struggle for freedom, and independence.

To represent the harmonious unification of two antagonistic sides, the worshippers run up and down the temple, switching constantly from left to right—from the female to the male side—to the sounds of drums and a sacred zither.

Near Libreville, Gabon

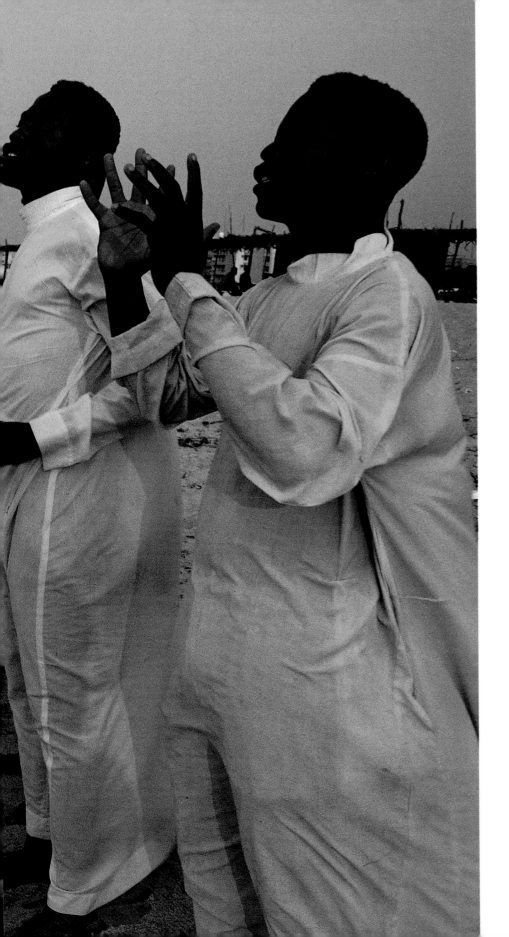

THE SOCIETY OF CHERUBIM AND SERAPHIM

Every Sunday afternoon, members of the Society of Cherubim and Seraphim, an independent African church, gather together on the beach for long sessions of prayer and singing. The Cherubim and Seraphim always dress in white and consider themselves extensions of God's hand on earth. Their form of evangelization can be somewhat aggressive, as they believe they are the only genuine Christians. They follow a literal, fundamentalist reading of the Bible, emphasizing the role of the Holy Ghost and Jesus as savior and healer. Many members join this church in search of solutions to problems or cures for illness, as their prophets promise rapid miracle solutions. The services are often very lively and emotional, with worshippers giving exuberant expression to their faith as a way to forget their daily troubles.

Lagos, Nigeria

155

WESTERNERS ARE FLAWED

These worshippers are preparing for Sunday mass at the Society of Cherubim and Seraphim, a church founded just after the First World War. The war had surprising ramifications in Africa: it revealed to the population that white-skinned people were neither invulnerable nor infallible. This new view of whites was first felt in the local population's approach to religion— maybe God was not white after all; maybe He was black.

In the 1920s, prophetic Aladura churches flourished in southern Nigeria. Joseph Ayo Babalola, a simple road builder, had a waking dream in which God ordered him to preach the gospel. At first he was thought to be insane. After a brief period of internment, he began to travel throughout Nigeria and Ghana, drawing crowds and holding healing sessions wherever he went. Babalola preached for a Christian awakening, attacking traditional religion, forbidding polygamy, and burning fetishes, idols, and other objects associated with witchcraft. He founded the Society of Cherubim and Seraphim after an influenza epidemic, persuading his followers to seek cures through prayer. This belief in miracle cures was at the heart of the church. After Babilola's death, the church continued to grow. At the beginning of the twenty-first century, it has some six hundred thousand members, as well as two seminaries, twenty-six secondary schools, its own teacher-training college, and missionaries throughout West Africa and in the United States.

Lagos, Nigeria

A MYSTICAL ACROBAT

This young Yacouba girl is a snake dancer. Young initiates who study this ritual dance are now few and far between. In western Ivory Coast, the snake dance precedes a display of masks. The dance is as spectacular as it is dangerous. A male dancer throws the girl, spinning, into the air. He holds up his dagger as if to impale her, dropping it at the very last moment as she wraps herself round his waist. He throws three initiates each time he dances, ending up with the three girls wrapped round him like a belt.

Ivory Coast

THE MARKS OF GOD

This girl is five years old. She has been in seclusion in a Vodun convent on the border between Benin and Togo for three months. On her forehead is the sign of the sacred rope that unites all the followers of Hevieso. As a novice, she must undergo obligatory ritual scarification to mark the end of her initiation period. An old woman uses a pocket knife to cut small incisions, which are rubbed with herbs, ashes, and a dark red paste. This mix enters the skin and leaves blackish stains, specific to her convent, on the child's cheeks. The woman also cuts a "necklace" of little scars that start from her shoulder, traverse her back, and cross under her chest. This is the sign of the rope of Hevieso, the god of thunder. The little girl remained silent throughout the operation, not giving any signs of pain.

In addition to the ritual scars, the girl has tattoos. On her right arm is a tattoo of the bell rung by the vodun to express joy and anger, and on her left arm is the double sign of Sofia, the sacred ax, which protects vodun-si from evil.

Mono region, Benin

VODUN, A RELIGION OF LIFE

These worshippers of Mami Wata, goddess of water and the ocean, have been prepared to follow the goddess since they were born. The Vodun religion acts as a guide to life based on the realities of African societies. It puts women at the heart of nature and society, and can be adapted according to different situations, seasons, climates, and eras. Nothing disappears; everything is reborn, in nature and in society. There is continuity between these vodun-si and their ancestors.

This religion is based on an understanding of the world as a spiritual chain between the living, the dead, the deities, and Mawu, the supreme being. Humans are immortal thanks to the reincarnation of souls and the rebirth of generations. This notion leads to the celebration both of life and of death, which is held to be the beginning of life in the afterworld. This optimistic view of eternity shapes society and the moral framework of Vodun, which aims to make women happy on earth before their souls go to their rest in the realm of the ancestors. This pragmatic approach is different from Christianity, which is based on the belief that humans are not on earth to be happy, but to work towards salvation in the afterlife.

Togo

DANGEROUS XHOSA INITIATION RITES

One of these two young Xhosa men, from one of the principal ethnic groups in South Africa, is wearing a lamb's wool and feather headdress typical of initiation rites. Once the ceremony is over, the hut, blankets, and other objects used by the boys will be burned. During the ritual, the initiates will be circumcised. This delicate operation is often carried out with unsterilized blades, which can lead to serious infection. Every year, several hundred young Xhosa men fall ill or even die during the initiation period.

Transkei, South Africa

CIRCUMCISION AS A RITE OF PASSAGE

From late fall to early spring, the Xhosa of South Africa undergo their initiation. The young men go to stay in an isolated hut, where they are circumcised. They must also undergo demanding physical tests, such as being subjected to a period of extreme frugality to test their endurance and their willpower. When the period of isolation comes to an end, they perform a dance imitating bulls, and continue dancing until they are exhausted, in order to free themselves of the stress of the initiation period. All young men must undergo initiation to become a man. If anyone fails to complete the rituals, he will be seen as weak for his entire life and no respectable woman will agree to be his wife.

Transkei, South Africa

WOMAN-GODDESS

This women is in a trance, and wears a white kaolin clay mask to represents her ritual death. She no longer has control over her acts, voice, or movements. An orisha possesses her free soul, the only part of the individual that the deity can possess. Her second soul, the vital soul, which controls her physical body, automatically obeys the orisha's whims and, for a brief while, the woman becomes a goddess. For some forty minutes, the orisha transmits his wishes and gives advice to the congregation. Once the message has been transmitted, the deity withdraws from the woman's body. Her free soul returns, and she wakes from her trance. Such trances can last anywhere from a few minutes to several hours, or even a whole day and night. There are no rules: orishas and voduns are unpredictable beings.

Togo

SEEING IS BELIEVING

The Bwiti initiation ritual lasts several weeks, during which the initiate lives secretly in the forest, away from his community. His physically demanding daily routine is designed to purify him and test his powers of endurance. He is forced to pray naked in the forest several times a night before being whipped with branches dipped in boiling water. The supreme test at the end of the initiation period is the journey to the realm of the dead to meet the Bwiti. For this, the initiate lies on a bed of leaves and chews a piece of iboga bark to "open his mind." The drug contained in the bark takes him on a "journey," which begins with a violent bout of vomiting. After ten or so hours, he begins to see vague, blurry, incoherent images, followed by visions of strange, aggressive animals. He is accompanied on his journey by a priest playing hypnotic music on a sacred zither. The initiate feels himself sliding into clouds, then into a marvelous world filled with light, where he is met by an extraordinary figure who welcomes him to the village of the dead. The figure then transforms into a ball of unbearably dazzling light, crying "I am the master of the world, I am Bwiti!" and the initiation is complete.

Libreville region, Gabon

THE FELA SHRINE

The great Nigerian musician Fela Anikulapokuti called the hall where he gave concerts a shrine, as a way of reminding people of the spiritual dimension of music. In the 1980s, he never performed without his mystical mentor, the Professor, who made a ritual sacrifice in the middle of each concert. He killed a goat or a hen to exorcise the evil spirits that might attack the music.

Lagos, Nigeria

INITITATION CELEBRATIONS

Vodun-si from across the region hold a week-long celebration to mark the end of the initiation period, when the novices leave their convent. It is a chance for their families to demonstrate their wealth and prestige, and to compete in displays of sacred dances. On the last day, once the novices have undergone purification in the forest, they go to the main square in the village, singing and dancing. They make their way around the square seven times, then sit perched on earthenware jugs. If the jug breaks, it proves the girl has behaved badly, and she is disgraced. If the jug remains intact, the girl is welcomed into the Vodun religion, with festivities and dancing. Each new initiate performs a special dance, during which she dances for three or four minutes before changing her wrap—no fewer than forty times in the course of the afternoon.

Vogan region, Togo

THE SOUL-EATER

Germaine is sixty-two. She lives in Ivory Coast near the border with Burkina Faso. Her face and part of her body bear traces of leprosy, and because of this she is feared by the inhabitants of her village. No one dares greet her or sell her food, and it is believed that, at night, she turns into a bat to eat the souls of her victims, sucking their vital energy until they die of anemia.

According to local beliefs, soul-eaters gather together in secret societies of nine, seventeen, twenty-five, or thirty members. To join, each member must sacrifice a member of their family, which will then give them the power to turn into animals to kill their victims.

This belief in animal transformation is fairly widespread throughout Africa. In a recent case in Ivory Coast, a man killed a friend with a machete. He explained to the police that the two of them were walking in the forest, when his friend turned into a lion and he was obliged to kill him to avoid being eaten. No one in his village questioned his story.

Ivory Coast

THE END OF THE WORLD IS NIGH

The spiritual community of the prophet of Kokangba lives in northern Ivory Coast. The prophet lives at the top of a mountain, as far away from the sea as possible, for safety, because he is convinced that the Apocalypse is near. He believes that the flood mentioned in the Bible will be a giant tsunami that will engulf the whole world, and that God has given him the mission of saving mankind from extinction. Like Noah, he has gathered his believers and some domesticated animals and is building an ark on the mountain. In preparation for the Apocalypse, he takes the confessions of those who are to be saved, who must be free from all sin.

Near Daloa, Ivory Coast

POLYGAMY AND THE HARRIST FAITH

Harrism, founded in the early twentieth century by William Harris, is the most influential syncretic religion in Ivory Coast. It is based on Christianity, and among its tenets are a belief in one God, love of one's neighbor, public confession, and the glorification of baptism. Harrists preach the destruction of fetishes and witchcraft, and condemn lying, theft, alcohol, and adultery. Polygamy, however, is tolerated.

Harrism has been an official religion in Ivory Coast since 1961, along with Catholicism, Protestantism, and Islam. Today, Harrism is also followed in Liberia and Ghana.

Ivory Coast

ALBERT ATCHO, THE DEVIL'S CONFESSOR

Like Christ, the prophet Albert Atcho lives with twelve disciples, in Bingerville, Ivory Coast. He believes God has given him a sacred mission to fight the devil. His reputation is such that people come from all over the country to seek his help with problems believed to be caused by witchcraft, such as missing children, thefts, or mysterious crimes that can only be the work of black magic. Albert Atcho unmasks witches by organizing "confessions for the devil" or "confessions in double." This ritual enacts the life of those who have come to consult him. A veritable psychodrama takes place, during which the voice and gestures of the participant change as he or she assumes two separate personas, becoming both victim and criminal. In a terrible voice, he accuses himself of being the devil, guilty of all crimes. In this way Albert Atcho publicly identifies the witch, who is possessed by an evil spirit. Unusually, and unlike other African customs where the guilty party is put to death, no one is punished as a result of Albert Atcho's rituals.

Near Bingerville, Ivory Coast

SHANGO PUNISHES WITH LIGHTNING

This young Vodun-si is in the service of Shango, god of thunder and lightning, in the form of the king of Oyo in Nigeria. During storms, every clap of thunder is met with shouts of "Long live the king!" The worshipper's clothes are in the deity's colors: the white cowries—the shells formerly used for currency—and the red on her hands representing impure blood symbolize both calm and anger, indicating that Shango is just, but can be moved to violence when angered.

Shango is believed to be responsible for deaths by lightning, and those he strikes down are held to be criminals or witches. Their bodies are thrown far from the village and quickly forgotten. Deprived of a religious burial, the soul of the deceased is condemned to wander in limbo for all eternity, and will never be reincarnated.

Nigeria

NOLI, LAND OF GHOSTS

The black mud that these young girls from Togo have smeared on their hair and the color of their clothes indicate that they belong to the Vodun community of the sacred forest of Be in Lome. This religion dates back to the earliest Ewe settlements during the late sixteenth century, when the Ewe moved here from the neighboring Yoruba country. In rituals, this part of Nigeria is deemed the cradle of the ancestors and is known as Noli (the Ghost). The land to the east of Togo is the home of the rising sun, where the souls of the dead repose after crossing the coast of death.

Sacred forest of Be, Lome, Togo

FEAR OF WITCHCRAFT

This woman lives in a small village near Port Saint Johns, in Transkei. She wears the traditional garb and makeup of a Xhosa woman of her region. However, two years ago, a Pentecostal church was set up near her home and certain members of the congregation threatened to accuse her of witchcraft if she carried on wearing her makeup. It is not uncommon for Fundamentalist Christians to spread rumors of witchcraft in order to bring in new worshippers, convincing them that their problems are due to supernatural causes. For example, many people believe AIDS is a *muti* made by a witch. The virus and the body's immune system are a metaphor for witchcraft and ritual protection.

Since the end of the apartheid era, the black population of South Africa has been in a spiritual crisis, as illustrated by this fear of witchcraft.

Transkei, South Africa

THE SABER PROTECTS
THE ASHANTO CHIEF

The saber plays an important role in moments of crisis for the Ashanti of Ghana. Here, it will ensure a good life in the realm of the dead for a recently deceased chief, thanks to the magic force of the talismans sealed into its handle.

The magnificence and splendor of Ashanti funerals depend on the status and wealth of the deceased. Gold jewelry, symbolizing power, is displayed on the body for the guests to admire. During the funeral, young girls perform ritual dances representing the hope of perpetuating the deceased person's lineage. Women are held to have the power to console the bereaved and soothe their grief, and dance and movement symbolize the return of life.

Ghana

AKAN GOLD

These ceremonial glasses are made of solid gold. Gold was of great religious importance for the Akan and their neighboring tribe, the Ashanti. In the past, when an Akan king died, his eyes and ears were filled with gold powder and a packet of gold was placed in his coffin. These glasses, however, no longer symbolize religion, but the tribal chief's nobility and wealth. Such displays of wealth and power are increasingly rare.

Ivory Coast

TWO SOULS

These Bantu women believe that life consists of four elements: Nitu (the body), Menga (the blood), Moyo (the principal soul), and Mfumu Kutu (the soul's double, or personality). Life as a whole is Zina (a perfect being). At night, while the body sleeps, the double of the soul wanders in the wild, and its experiences in the bush result in the sleeper's dreams. If the sleeper finds it hard to wake up in the morning, it is because Mfumu Kutu has not yet returned from its nightly wandering.

This second soul dwells in the ear and is therefore known as "Lord of the Ear." It is lent to man by God for the duration of his lifetime and taken back after death. The principal soul, on the other hand, journeys to the depths of the ocean after death, where the ancestors have their houses and fields, and where they hunt game. (For the Bantu, water is an essential part of life. Water spirits control magic forces and are used in protective talismans.)

After a sojourn in the ocean, Moyo is chosen by God to become a deity.

Democratic Republic of Congo

MASKS AS PROTECTION

The Lord's Resistance Army (LRA) is a rebel movement that was founded in Uganda in 1988. Joseph Kony, leader of the LRA, led the rebellion to establish a theocratic Christian regime based on a fundamentalist reading of the Bible. Some two million people were forced from their homes during this conflict and now live in extreme poverty in refugee camps.

The LRA is accused of numerous war crimes, including kidnapping as many as twenty thousand children to force them into combat and sexual slavery. Eighty percent of the LRA's forces are child soldiers. Every night, some forty thousand children flee their villages to avoid being kidnapped. They survive by begging on the side of the road, wearing masks and trinkets supposed to give them ritual protection.

Near Kampala, Uganda

180

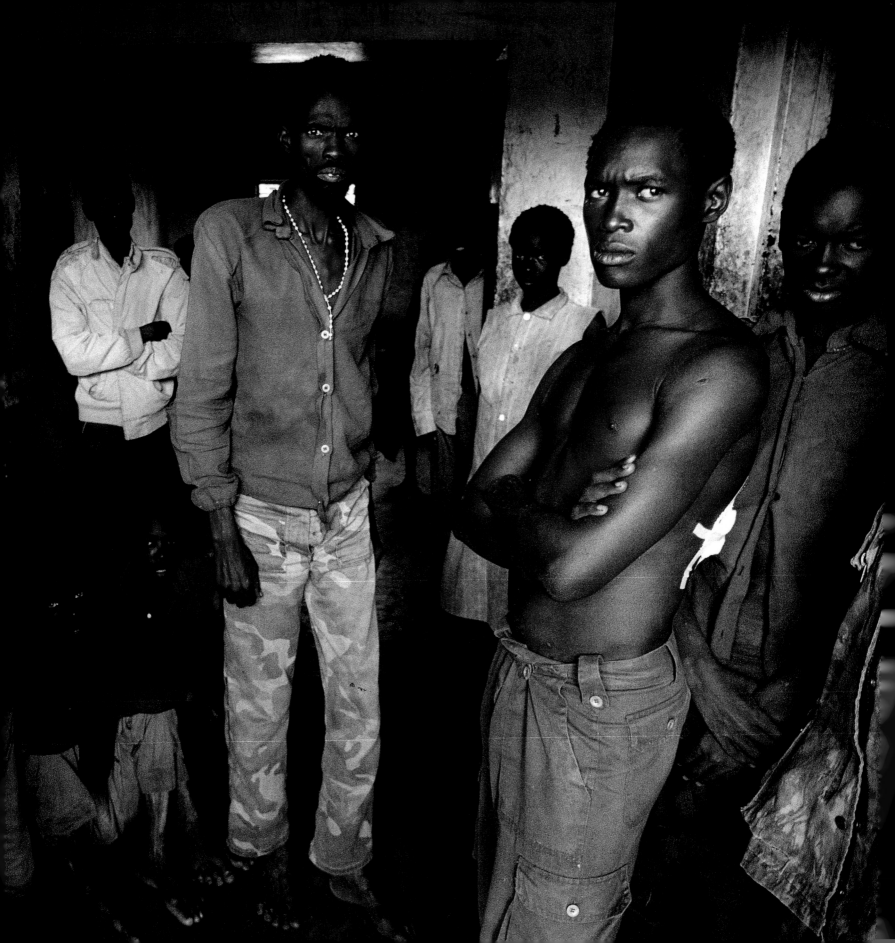

HOLY WATER, HOLY BULLETS

In Uganda, all that remains of the Holy Spirit Movement is this group of starving men in a Kampala prison. All the others have joined the Lord's Resistance Army. In the 1980s, a young Acholi woman by the name of Alice Auma, aged around thirty, claimed she had received a sacred mission from a spirit called Lakwena to create an army to overthrow the Ugandan government. She became known as Alice Lakwena, or the African Joan of Arc. She was obsessed with the spiritual purity of her soldiers, who had to undergo a purification ritual before joining her. Before each battle, she sprinkled the soldiers with holy water as protection against bullets, claiming that the bullets would liquefy before hitting the soldiers. Any soldier who died in combat was accused of failing to obey the twenty commandments she imposed on her followers. After the total defeat of her army in November 1987, Alice Auma left for Kenya, where she eventually died in a refugee camp.

Kampala, Uganda

MYSTIC AFRICA

A woman with her face painted with sacred white kaolin clay crosses the street in Lagos. Such reminders of the deeply spiritual nature of life in Africa are everywhere. Although the African continent is also home to the world's major religions, traditional beliefs are still held. Many Africans think of the gods as soon as they wake up, and throughout the day are constantly aware of their presence. They believe that every aspect of their social, emotional, and professional life depends on the goodwill of the gods and that sickness and disease also have supernatural causes.

Lagos, Nigeria

page 187

LAGOS, CAPITAL OF MIRACLES

This little girl, ill since birth, is unable to walk. She is cared for by parishioners of the Chrislamherb Church, the Islamic church of Christ, whose doctrine incorporates a mixture of Christianity, Islam, and mysticism. It is one of the thousands of charismatic churches that flourish in Lagos. Every Sunday, the preacher, Alhaji Alfa, organizes a session of miracles. Using the Bible and the power of prayer he aims to cure this little girl, but after many attempts she is still unable to hold herself upright and is supported in the arms of the faithful. In Africa, miracles are a profitable business and can make fortunes for the unscrupulous.

Lagos, Nigeria

THE COST OF TAKING PHOTOGRAPHS

Daniel Lainé

Togo. September 1978. In a corner of the room, Kokué, a priestess in the service of Mami Wata, is sprinkling herself with eau de Cologne. She is a large woman with a cheerful expression and a deep, loud voice. She laughs a lot. Everything about her is ample—her gestures, her clothes, her body, and her generosity. The altar of her Vodun convent is heaped with a surprising jumble of objects—plastic dolls, soft toys, bottles, and a plaster statuette of the Virgin Mary lie next to a statue of Shiva. It is suffocatingly hot. An old fan spins lazily in the humid air. Kokué wipes the sweat from her forehead and gives my friend Etienne a knowing look, saying, "Has he brought everything? The bottle of schnapps? The white chicken? The candles? And 8,000 CFA francs?" Etienne nods. "So we can begin."

She takes my hands, closes her eyes, and utters sacred words in a mysterious language. Kokué's expression is serious and portentous as she calls on the Voduns to protect me. Etienne explains that she does not do this for just anyone, but she likes me and wants to carry out this ceremony of spiritual protection personally so that everything goes well for me in Africa. She chants the ritual words and casts cowrie shells on a mat. Her tone lightens and she reads the Fa oracle in a cheerful voice, shouting with laughter. Etienne looks on with respect.

What is happening? The situation is bizarre, embarrassing. I don't believe in God, nor in shamans and demons, and yet here I am, worried about the outcome. I don't believe in Vodun either but, all the same, I'm beginning to find the ambience unsettling. The priestess pours a little schnapps on the floor, then drinks from the bottle before handing it to me to do the same. The alcohol tastes strong and acrid. I am seized with shivers; burning hot but strangely reassured. Kokué sprinkles talcum powder on a bracelet of yellow, blue, and white beads, and then, with a sudden jerk, she snaps the chicken's neck, pouring its blood over the beads and throwing them on the floor. She explains to Etienne that they have fallen in a very good position, chuckling as she exclaims, "The white man is lucky!" She quickly slides the bracelet over my wrist. The stickiness of the chicken's blood stains my skin, making me feel nauseous. Kokué continues her strange prayer, pulling me towards her in a tight embrace. I look into her eyes as she presses her forehead against mine. Her every word reverberates in me like an echo. Suddenly, it is as though we are lost in a light fog—I feel an instant of dazed confusion, then nothing.

We are in a nightclub. An electric blue light shines on the face of a girl dancing on the deserted dance floor. Normally the nightclubs of Lome are packed on Sunday. I stare at her, not in an unpleasant or threatening manner, but with eyes shining with conviction. Her name is Colette and she is the most beautiful girl in the world. Her face is lovely, but sad, and she walks over to me boldly. I feel the softness of her skin, her warmth, and her smell, a mixture of sweat and spicy perfume. Her waist is so slender, so perfect. She

smiles at me but her smile does not reach her eyes. I must kiss her gently not to scare her. She unsettles me, like the music pouring from the loudspeakers.

What is the mystery of Vodun? Why has this girl come to me in the middle of the ritual?

The spell weakens and dissolves and I hear Kokué's hoarse voice reverberating through my brain. The priestess relinquishes her hold over me and looks into my eyes, laughing loud and long. Then she exclaims, "Mami Wata is pleased. Now you are at home here, Daniel!"

Vodun is a journey of sensuality and mystery. From that day on, I have felt at home in Africa. Ever since, I have traveled the continent enthusiastically, seeking out mysterious rituals, great soothsayers, and mad priests.

Lome. September 1980. A Tron Vodun ceremony. Three hundred people sit in a circle in a great courtyard. In the center is a flagpole bearing red and black flags. It is hot. The women dance and laugh and boys flirt desultorily with girls. People call out my name, happy to see me. Large men, muscles bulging, beat out a frantic rhythm on the drums; children join in, drumming furiously. Suddenly, the rhythm changes; people's expressions become somber. A cry tears the air, then another, and a woman falls to the floor in convulsions. She screams at the sky. A man jumps into the air, panting heavily, his eyes glazed. Three other men try to calm him in vain, as he jumps around the congregation. Other women fall into trances, gesticulating at each other. After a few minutes, they leave to change outside the courtyard, returning wearing red, white, and black shirts, with their faces smeared with kaolin. The atmosphere is now relaxed, as the women, possessed by capricious gods, harangue the good-natured crowd and make them laugh. The women are happy to let me take photographs, and then one of them, with an air of challenge, hands me a gourd of tafia, a rough, acrid alcohol. In an instant, the mood is one of religious ecstasy and the tempo accelerates. The ambience overtakes me; the blend of alcohol, music, and laughter is so true, so vital. In the heat of the African night, this festive atmosphere is reassuring. It evokes a fleeting harmony , which goes beyond the real and makes African communities so splendid.

I take photographs with my old, second-hand Nikon and cheap film. I don't have much money, but in Africa everyone shares, and I take comfort in my occasional poverty. Otherwise, how could I hope to understand the poverty that has this continent in a stranglehold? During this celebration I instinctively feel that I must not break the spell: no more photographs; they are violent, aggressive, pitiless. When I take photos, I hate myself, and I want to stop, to be there just for the beauty of the moment, not for the pictures. Yet it is at that precise instant that photography reveals its grandeur: such moments of doubt, of extreme self-questioning, create great images. To understand, you have to have lived such moments, when certainties are thrown into doubt and you are paralyzed with anxiety. How freeing it is just to stop, to put down the Nikon, to sit and dare to live for the instant. What a huge, dirty, unnatural effort to keep going at any cost, to take photos when you are cut off not only

from other people, but also from your own conscience. Photography has its dark, unpleasant, ugly, unhealthy side.

At the end of the night, a little drunk, I watch the people around me gesticulating, shouting, praying, and laughing. Where do they get their energy from? It is the vital energy of real life. I observe Vodun, Bwiti, and most other African religions as though they are theater performances, featuring gods alongside men, the dead performing with the living. The show is different every time, and I never tire of it. Eventually, the gods are sated and return to their homes. The men are exhausted and begin to leave, their voices dying away in the dark. The silence and the ocean air caress my face and I look at the tall coconut palms leaning gently over the road.

I must mention the thousands of miles I have traveled in bush taxis driving at breakneck speed, squashed in between a terrified student and a snoozing local woman. The drivers are not scared of their bald tires and spongy brakes; their gods will protect them. Not me. I have spent literally hundreds of hours on the road to meet the "black gods," with my stomach knotted in fear, haunted by the vision of my twisted, bloody body in a crushed heap of metal on the side of the road. I want to shout at the driver to slow down, but who dares show his fear and weakness?

No one knows Africa until they have experienced its difficulties: crushing heat, constant noise, poverty. Walking in a midday sun that weighs on you like lead. The noise of cars, their horns blaring. Pollution. Suspicion in the eyes of passers-by. The endless, white, aggressive light from which nothing can hide. Africa can be harsh. But then it is late afternoon, and the sun sinks towards the horizon. The air is filled with perfume from the trees and a refreshing breeze blows in from the ocean. Life becomes more serene. People share a beer in a local bar and listen to African pop music. Soon, night falls, sensual and magical. Africa's gods will soon walk among men once more.

VODUN FETISHES

Feitico means "objects made by a magician" in Portuguese, and is the origin of the term "fetish." In the past, Westerners referred to all objects containing a spirit used in the Animist faith as fetishes. They believed that Africans worshipped statues, stones, trees, animals, and rivers, and that the African gods inhabited objects. This simplistic understanding of African religions is outdated. Ethnologists now understand that most African religions are monotheistic and that fetishes are no more than temporary receptacles for spirits and Vodun deities. They represent the visible face of the gods and the place where sacrifices and offerings are made. This explains the dark color of these Vodun fetishes in a Lome shrine: they are covered in the dried blood, feathers, and fur of the animals sacrificed here.

Lome, Togo

Le Bris, Michel, ed. *Vaudou, exposition presenté à l'Abbaye de Daoulas*. Paris: Hoebeke, 2003.

Afrique méridionale. Atlas, 1978.

Aig-Imoukhuede, Frank. *Nigerian Culture*. Lagos:1991.

Akoun, André. *Afrique noire: mythes et croyances du monde*. Turnhout: Brépols, 1985.

Alexandre, Pierre. *Les Africains*. Turnhout: Brépols, 1982.

Arnaut, Robert. *L'Afrique du jour et de la nuit*. Paris: Presses de la Cité, 1978.

Arts du Nigeria. Paris: Réunion des musées nationaux. 1997.

Awolalu J., Omosade. *West African Traditional Religion*. Ibadan: Onibonoje Press, 1979.

Balandie, Georges. *Dictionnaire des civilisations africaines*. Paris: Fernand Hazan, 1968.

Balogun, Ola. "Nigeria." *Jeune Afrique*, 1978.

Camara, S. *Paroles très anciennes ou le mythe de l'accomplissement de l'homme*.
        Grenoble: La pensée sauvage, 1982.

Chesi, Gert. *Vaudou*. Paris: Fournier, 1982.

Cissé, Y. "Le sacrifice chez les Bambaras et les Malinké," in *Cahiers Systèmes de pensée en
        Afrique noire* 5. Paris: Centre National de la Recherche Scientifique, 1982.

Dmochowski, Z. R. *South-Eastern Nigeria*. London: Ethnographica, 2000.

Fadipe, N. A. *The Sociology of Yoruba*. Ibadan: Ibadan University Press, 1972.

Faïk-Nzuji, Clémentine M. *La Puissance du sacré*. Tournai: La Renaissance du livre, 2003.

Fortes, M. *Systèmes politiques africains*. Paris: Presses Universitaires de France, 1964.

Hebga, Meinrad P. *Sorcellerie*. Abidjan: Inades, 1979.

Henning, Christoph and Oberländer Hans. *Vaudou*. Koln: Taschen, 1996.

Herskovits, Melville J. *Dahomey, An Ancient West African Kingdom*. 2 vols.
        Evanston: Northwestern University Press, 1991.

Heusch, Luc de. *Objets signes d'Afrique*. Ghent: Snoeck, Ducaju et Zoon, 1994.

Histoire générale de l'Afrique. Paris: Unesco, 1998.

Hountondji, P. J. *Sur la philosophie africaine: critique de l'éthnophilosophie*. Paris: Maspero, 1977.

Koudolo Svetlana. *Institutions d'Afa et du Vodu*. DIFOP, 1991.

Le Bris, Michel, ed. *Vaudou, exposition presenté à l'Abbaye de Daoulas*. Paris: Hoebeke, 2003.

Magubane, Peter. *Vanishing Cultures of South Africa*. Cape Town: Struik, 1998.

Maupoil, B. *La Géomancie à l'ancienne côte des Esclaves*. Paris: Institut d'ethnologie, 1988.

Mdoufoume, Tsira Mdong. *Le Mvett, épopée Fang*. Paris: Présence Africaine, 1970.

Mertens, Alice, and Joan Broster. *African Elegance*. Cape Town: Purnell, 1973.

Morris, Jean, and Ben Levitas. *Tribal Life Today*. Cape Town: The College Press, 1987.

Müller, Klaus E., and Ute Ritz-Müller. *Afrique, la magie dans l'âme*. Köln: Könemann, 2000.

Mworoha, Émile. *Peuples et rois de l'Afrique des lacs*.
        Dakar and Abidjan: Nouvelles Éditions Africaines, 1977.

Nathan, T., and L. Hounkpatin. *La Parole de la forêt initiale*. Paris: Odile Jacob, 1996.
        Republished in paperback as *La Guérison Yoruba*, Paris: Odile Jacob, 1998.

Ortigues M.-C., and E. Ortigues. *Œdipe africain*. Paris: L'Harmattan, 1984.

Palau Marti, Montserrat. *Le Roi-dieu au Bénin*. Paris: Berger-Levrault, 1964.

Quenum, M. *Au pays des Fons, us et coutumes du Dahomey*.
        Paris: Maisonneuve et Larose, 1999.

———. *Us et coutumes du Dahomey*. Paris: Maisonneuve et Larose, 1983.

Rachewiltz, Boris de. *Éros noir*. Paris: La Jeune Parque, 1965.

Raponda Walker, André. *Rites et croyances des peuples du Gabon*. Paris: Présence Africaine, 1995.

Rivière, Claude. *Anthropologie religieuse des Eve du Togo*. Dakar and Abidjan:
        Nouvelles Éditions Africaines, 1981.

Sarpong, Peter. *Ghana in Retrospect*. Ghana Publishing Corporation, 1991.

Saulnier, A. *Anthologie du chant moderne en Afrique centrale*. L'Harmattan, 1993.

———. *Bangui raconte, contes de Centrafrique*. Paris: L'Harmattan, 2000.

———. *Le Centrafrique, entre mythe et réalité*. Paris: L'Harmattan, 1998.

———. *Plantes médicinales et soins en Centrafrique*. Saint-Maur: Sépia, 1998.

Savary, C. *La Pensée symbolique des Fò du Dahomey: tableau de la société et étude de la
        littérature orale d'expression sacrée dans l'ancien royaume du Dahomey*.
        Geneva: Médecine et Hygiène, 1976.

Stamm, A. *Histoire de l'Afrique précoloniale*. Paris: Presses Universitaires de France, 1997.

———. *La parole est un monde*. Paris: Le Seuil, 1999.

———. *Les Religions africaines*. Paris: Presses Universitaires de France, 1995.

Verger, P. *Dieux d'Afrique*. Paris: Hartman, 1954.

———. *Orisha: les dieux yorubas en Afrique et au Nouveau Monde*. Paris: Métailié, 1983.

Zahan, D. *Religion, spiritualité et pensée africaines*. Paris: Payot, 1970.

Notes

1. "While Mousso Koroni and Pemba were committing their acts, the smell stank in the surrounding air as it rose, and by the time it reached God it had nearly spoiled, corrupted and destroyed the universe. To avoid the destruction of the world, his creation, God went to the uppermost of his seven heavens and seven earths and, with a bolt of lightning, sacrificed a ram that he had hastily created using the dense matter of which heaven is made, *ma kaba*. This ram, called *dyigi makan dyigi* (the eminent ram of the eminent master of the heavens) or *son saka* (sacrificial ram) had a white body and black limbs, neck, and head. On its forehead was a white star, which gave it its third name, *doolo saka* (the starred ram). The ram's blood flowed down the paths of the *banan ngolo*, from the seventh to the first heaven, cleansing, purifying, and energizing the whole universe." Youssouf Cissé, "Le sacrifice chez les Bambaras et les Malinkés," *Cahiers Systèmes de pensée en Afrique noire* 5: 68-69.

2. *Religion, spiritualité et pensée africaines* (Paris: Payot, Bibliothèque scientifique, 1970).

3. M.-C. and E. Ortigues, *Œdipe africain* (Paris: L'Harmattan, 1984).

4. *Sê* means both "fate" and "God," the source of individual destinies, in Fon, Gun, and Ewe.